Our Laundry, Our Town

OUR LAUNDRY, OUR TOWN

My Chinese American Life from Flushing to the Downtown Stage and Beyond

Alvin Eng

EMPIRE STATE EDITIONS

AN IMPRINT OF FORDHAM UNIVERSITY PRESS

NEW YORK 2022

Excerpt from *World Without End* © 1989 Holly Hughes,
courtesy of the author.

Copyright © 2022 Alvin Eng

Fordham University Press has no responsibility for the persistence
or accuracy of URLs for external or third-party Internet websites referred
to in this publication and does not guarantee that any content on such
websites is, or will remain, accurate or appropriate.

Fordham University Press also publishes its books in a variety of electronic
formats. Some content that appears in print may not be available
in electronic books.

Visit us online at www.fordhampress.com/empire-state-editions.

Library of Congress Cataloging-in-Publication Data available online
at https://catalog.loc.gov.

Printed in the United States of America

24 23 22   5 4 3 2 1

First edition

For Wendy,
the best days and best work of my life
have come by your side.
Thank you for taking my hand
and still holding it.

In loving memory of Jeff Chan.
Asian American studies and literature pioneer.
A singular friend, mentor and inspiration.
Rest in power.

CONTENTS

Our Laundry, Our Town

Chapter 1

The Urban Oracle Bones of Our Laundry

Channeling China's Last Emperor and Rock 'n' Roll's First Opera

WHILE I HAVE been blessed to have always had a roof over my head and the honor of living with loved ones, when I was growing up, homelessness was a constant spiritual state. A child's longing to belong is one of the most powerful forces and relentless muses on Earth. In every culture, belonging has many different nuances of meaning and resonance. What and who exactly constitutes that destination of longing changes with every age and, in childhood, with every grade. What never seems to change is the feeling that we never quite arrive, and when or if we do, it only lasts for a fleeting time and was never quite what we expected.

These memoir portraits are an attempt to decode and process the urban oracle bones from growing up as the youngest of five children in an immigrant Chinese family that ran a hand laundry. Our family was born of an arranged marriage, and our laundry was in the Flushing, Queens, neighborhood of that singular universe that was New York City in the 1970s. Like many children of immigrant or "other" family origins in late-twentieth-century America, I was constantly seeking American frames of reference with which to contextualize my own "outsider" experiences and sensibilities.

I was born in Flushing on May 24, 1962, in the long-since-shuttered Parsons Hospital at the corner of Parsons Boulevard and 35th Avenue. May 24 is also the birthday of Bob Dylan; Patti LaBelle; Tommy Chong of the 1970s stoner comedy team "Cheech & Chong"; and Queen Victoria; and the anniversary of the day that the Brooklyn Bridge was first opened to traffic in 1883. One of Flushing's most famous icons, the New York Mets, was also born in 1962.

Although Flushing became New York City's second China-town during the 1980s, a.k.a. "The People's Republic of Floo-Shing," in the 1960s and '70s, we were one of only a fistful of Chinese families there. The Flushing of my childhood was still basking in the afterglow of the post–World War II suburban baby boom. That boom was celebrated at the 1964–65 World's Fair, held in Flushing Meadows Park. That World's Fair was the zenith of "The American Century," when anything was supposed to be possible. In this euphoric mood, Flushing immigrants were the last wave who gave up everything. They had forsaken their customs, their language—many would have changed their appearance if they could—just to get a whiff of "The American Dream."

The underside of growing up in the post–World War II euphoria of the World's Fair, as well as in the shadows of the Cold War, was that China was looming as Uncle Sam's Communist Public Enemy #2. Under this cloud, our laundry frequently became a target for salvos of verbal abuse like "Chinky Cho, Go Home!" As a child in this hostile milieu, I never envisioned even setting foot in China, let alone perform a memoir monologue, *The Last Emperor of Flushing*, there that I wrote in English based on my family. This monologue was inspired, in part, by Thornton Wilder's Americana play *Our Town*. I also never would have imagined that this Americana work has some Chinese artistic influence and roots.

Our "Foo J. Chin Chinese Hand Laundry" was a long, narrow railroad-styled store that stretched from a parking lot in the rear to Flushing's bustling Union Street in the front. Going from the back door to the front door, the way we entered every morning, the rear room was the family area—comprising a kitchen, dining, and napping area. This is where we all ate and where the kids did their homework and goofed off between laundry chores.

The middle room was where the ironing and wrapping of laundered garments took place. The middle room had long rectangular padded tables for ironing and sorting laundry and large white metal sewing stations. This was the largest room and also primarily the court of our mother, Toy Lain Chin Eng or "The Empress Mother" as she is anointed in *The Last Emperor of Flushing*. In this middle room, The Empress Mother took her breaks, read the Chinese newspapers, and listened to her beloved Cantonese opera records.

The front room was where our family, or what I, in my *Last Emperor of Flushing* persona, refer to as The Eng Dynasty, interacted with the outside world. After entering through the front door, customers stood behind a wall-to-wall wooden counter. This is where they dropped off their dirty laundry and later picked up and paid for their cleaned, wrapped laundry. Directly opposite our laundry's front door, the counter had a drawbridge of sorts—a cut-away countertop and gated swing door—to receive deliveries and children coming home from school. This was the smallest room and also the domain of our Dad, King Wah Eng. Between greeting customers and tending to all matters of laundry business, this is where he listened to *WCBS Newsradio 880* on his small transistor radio and read the *Daily News*. On most busy Saturdays, the entire family would be in this room tending to customers.

The middle and front room walls were lined with floor-to-ceiling shelves of rows and rows of brown paper–wrapped packages of the customers' clean laundry. Each brown paper package had a different colored ticket on the outside. In my child's mind's eye, each brightly colored ticket was a window into a different apartment of the big brown building represented by the shelves of wrapped laundry packages. The cleaned garments wrapped up in these packages were the silent witnesses to the events and rituals that made up the lives of their wearers. The wearers all belonged to families in which both parents did not work twelve hours a day, six days a week in a laundry. Instead, the father worked only five days a week, 9–5 in an office; the mother was a full-time stay-at-home Mom, and both of them spoke perfect English. I called this building "The Great Wall of Laundry."

My parents had a difficult, strained arranged marriage—one in which they were completely committed to the family unit but not so much to each other. They were both illegal immigrants from a tiny village outside of Toisan, a port city on the Pearl River delta in the southern China province of Guangdong, formerly known as Canton. Our family owned and operated a series of Foo J. Chin Chinese Hand Laundries—first in Hoboken, New Jersey, and then on East 86th Street on Manhattan's upper east side. The Flushing laundry was our family's third. In previous laundries, Gene, Jane, and Vic (siblings 1, 2, and 3, respectively) had another name and purpose for the "family area," or back room, of the laundry. They called this area home. They not only took their meals, did their homework, and played together between chores in the laundry's back room, they also bathed, slept, and dreamed there. My brother Herman and I (siblings 4 and 5) were the only Eng Dynasty children to not live our formative years in the back room or family area of the laundry. For our entire childhoods, we had the privilege of living in a private house that was separate from our laundry.

Because Dad spoke English and The Empress Mother did not, Dad's station in our laundry and in our family was on the front-line. Dad's was usually the first face customers would see as they entered the laundry. Always dressed in his white button-down shirt with a pen holder on the left front shirt pocket, he sat behind the front counter like a target and went eyeball to eyeball with each and every customer, hustler, and angry war veteran who walked through the door. People would routinely open the door and take pot shots like:

"Can you *speak-eee English-eee Chah-lee?*"

"No *tick-eee, no shirt-eee.*"

Dad would take one for the family and grow sullen and speechless. The Empress Mother, however, would respond to these taunts with a lusty:

"*Ai-yah! Moe-Yung Bok-Gwai, kare see um ben!*" . . . ["Useless white devil ghosts, you can step on shit and it will not bend!" Note: The author's informal phonetics appear throughout the book.]

This, as translated from the delicate Toisan dialect of Cantonese, surely one of the overlooked romance languages of the twentieth century.

The Empress Mother's station in our laundry and in our family abutted the wall that divided the front room public business space from the private family space. Because The Empress Mother could stay behind my Dad, she got to keep her fiery Toisan core together.

From the late nineteenth to the late twentieth century, 80 percent of Chinese immigrants to America emigrated from Toisan. During this time, Toisan was the dominant dialect and aesthetic of the Chinatowns and working-class Chinese communities throughout North America. In this light, and in that era, the Toisanese were very much like the Sicilians. Both groups were southern outcasts, mostly farmers, who were looked down upon as being too loud and belligerent, uncouth and uncultured, by their supposedly more sophisticated, governing northern brethren. Guangdong and Sicily are also geographically separated from their respective mainlands. Guangdong is isolated by a foreboding mountain range and until the early twentieth century was accessible only by sea. This separation and isolation instilled a staunch, independent spirit in its people. In North America, Toisantowns, like Sicilian enclaves, operated under their own rules, regulations, and justice systems. When words, deeds, and laws failed, there was always the meat cleaver.

While I never saw my parents pull actual meat cleavers on each other, I witnessed their weekly, sometimes daily, tremors of psychological warfare on each other grow more viciously antagonistic week after week. Inevitably, this led to an explosion.

One afternoon while in the third grade, I came home from school to find that Dad had pinned The Empress Mother to one of the padded ironing tables and was threatening to strike her.

"Dad, let her go!" I screamed.

"*Nee slee kie-ya!*" ["You stupid bastard!"] The Empress Mother shrieked.

"Shut up!" ordered Dad, and struck her.

I raced next door to Norman's T.V. repair shop.

"Please! Please! Help me! My parents are fighting!"

A repairman ran with me to the back of the laundry, where Dad was still striking Mom. Dad saw the repairman and immediately stopped.

"Hey," intervened the repairman. "Let's just take it easy here, all right."

After de-escalating this violent encounter, the repairman retreated back to his shop next door, leaving me alone with Dad and The Empress Mother. In the aftermath of this primal breach of trust, none of us could even look at each other. I gazed up at The Great Wall of Laundry and wished I could go home with one of those packages. To live with another family—one of those that unwrapped their packages and then wore the cleaned shirts, skirts, slacks, and ties.

Incidents like this left me petrified and scarred inside and out—reluctant to deal with conflict and confrontation on any level. I spent much of my childhood searching inward for psychological solace as well as physical protection. To escape the oft-times suffocating and intimidating environment of our laundry, thankfully my brother Herman and I bonded and created a joyous world of our own through the power of rock 'n' roll.

I bought my first vinyl record, a single, at age six. On the second floor of the Masters department store on the corner of Main Street and 37th Avenue in downtown Flushing, I somehow broke away from my older siblings and sprinted over to the music and records department. Barely able to reach the counter, I plopped my holiday or birthday one-dollar bill on the counter and said, "'Hey Jude' and 'Revolution' by The Beatles." The surprised clerk first looked to my older siblings, who had by now caught up to me, to confirm my purchase. They did. Just as I don't exactly remember how I had a one-dollar bill in my pocket, I also don't remember how I knew to ask for both songs of what I perceived to be a double A–sided single. I just did. My second record purchase one year later of a full LP album—a double LP, actually—forever changed and strongly influenced the futures of Herman and me.

Between the first and second record purchases, Gene, Jane, and Vic all moved out of the house. Hopefully, this was not in reaction to my rogue record purchase. Coincidentally, all three got married in the following year, 1970. Now, the immediate Flushing contingent of The Eng Dynasty consisted of The Empress Mother, Dad, Herman, and me. The first action that Herman took as its newly anointed oldest sibling was to talk me into pooling my saved laundry salary/allowance with his to purchase a "double album."

"Everybody on the block is talking about *Tommy*," raved Herman. "The Who are even gonna play the whole thing at Woodstock. We have to get it."

"But six bucks for one album?" I asked—now being the seasoned, suspicious music consumer.

"It's a double album, just like *The White Album*," Herman carefully presented his claim. "And it's only on sale at Korvettes—"

"Korvettes is so far away and it's pouring out!" I objected.

"It's eight plus tax at Record Spec or King Karol on Main Street," Herman rebutted.

"I don't know, Herm . . ."

"Al, we gotta do it . . . the rain's letting up . . . it'll be worth every cent. I promise," Herman made his closing argument.

"Oh . . . O.K."

I reluctantly handed over my hard-saved laundry salary/allowance to Herman, putting our combined kitty over the magic seven-dollar threshold (there was tax to pay on vinyl records, after all). Off we rode on our Schwinn banana-seat bikes through three neighborhoods and over ten miles roundtrip through a lighter but still steady rain, to E. J. Korvette in Douglaston—the only store in northeast Queens where we could afford to buy *Tommy*. As he would in so many instances throughout our life, Herman did the heavy lifting of tucking the double album inside his windbreaker to safely transport *Tommy* home.

After a deep listening to The Who's and rock 'n' roll's first opera—particularly to the transcendent "Listening to You" finale, a majestic moment where guru and disciple, Svengali and puppet, audience and artist are all united in one twelve-bar rock 'n' roll nirvana—*Tommy's* context became our context for . . . everything. Herman was right, it was worth every cent.

Herman and I started quoting the lyrics from *Tommy* to each other to the point where those lyrics became, virtually, our entire vocabulary. We wandered around Flushing and in Manhattan's Chinatown on Sundays with our parents and imagined connections between our two most familiar stomping grounds and The Who's native London neighborhood of Shepherd's Bush. After witnessing some heinous screaming match between Dad and The Empress Mother in our laundry or in Chinatown, Herman and I would instinctively turn to each other and talk/sing: "How do you think he does it?—I don't know . . ."

By mimicking the "Pinball Wizard" vocal interplay of *Tommy's* principal composer and The Who's guitarist, Pete Townshend, and Who lead vocalist, Roger Daltrey, we found a favorite new pastime. We also found a way to deflect some of life's unpleasantries with the mighty shield of rock 'n' roll.

The band members' British surnames, such as Townshend and Entwistle, rolled off our tongues and minds in a way that felt more organic to us than those of our relatives' names of Chin, Woo, Yee, or Wong. In a strange sense, The Who's names and neighborhoods and, of course, their music started to give

Herman and me a stronger sense of home than even our own names and home.

Herman's next big purchase involved his talking our parents into buying him a guitar from WBG Music on Roosevelt Avenue. On this guitar, he learned to play all of the songs from *Tommy*—setting him on a lifelong path that was guided by music. For me, *Tommy* launched a lifelong habit of constantly quoting rock lyrics—first as a fan and later as a music journalist and publicist and, even now, as a playwright, performer, and educator.

When we co-purchased *Tommy*, our five-year age difference was tenable as I was seven and Herman was twelve. By the time we became nine and fourteen, things were radically different. Herman started working outside of our laundry at the nearby Adventurer's Inn summer amusement park and year-round gaming arcade (and we're talking pinball). Honing their musical skills and feeling their teenage mojo, Herman and his friends were also slowly becoming neighborhood rock stars who were fully expecting to inherit The Who's mantle.

Now often alone with my parents in the laundry, I started relating less to The Who and more to the protagonist–title character of their first rock opera. Listening to *Tommy* and now drawing pictures became my sanctuary and inward escape from the domestic warfare being waged by my parents. Tommy is a "deaf, dumb, and blind pinball wizard" whose "miracle cure" makes him a hearing, seeing, and speaking international phenom. Of course, his parents manipulate his newfound and unsought fame for their own greed. Ultimately, Tommy retreats into his unreachable, deaf, dumb, and blind mode, as represented by the elegiac "See Me, Feel Me, Touch Me, Heal Me" motif.

While listening to *Tommy*, I often drew pencil portraits of my heroes from the New York Knicks, Mets, Giants, and, of course, The Who. Along with my drawing escape, I started becoming equally enthralled with *Tommy's* accompanying artwork and packaging. The album cover artwork smartly did not include photos of the band, as was common practice back then. As a result, the twelve-page booklet and triple foldout album cover created a 36″ × 12″ immersive gallery or hall of mirrors to which I always had access in the back room of our laundry.

My canvases were the coarse sheets of 24″ × 24″ white shipping paper packed atop and below the cleaned laundry within the voluminous number of boxes being shipped to the store . . . and let me come, ahem, clean here with a secret: During our family's three decades of operating the Foo J. Chin Chinese Hand Laundry from 1947–1977, no one ever hand washed a single piece of clothing—without an additional fee being charged.

Both Eng Dynasty "generations"—Gene, Jane, and Vic and then Herman and I—assisted our parents with the same primary laundry duties of sorting the customers' dirty laundry that was to be picked up and washed "outside" at the end of the day. When the clean laundry came back in a day or two, it was time to set about the massive job of collating the newly cleaned and pressed laundry into the customer's orders. Once we'd collated, we wrapped the cleaned clothes in those rectangular plain brown paper bundles that used to be ubiquitous on city streets and in outer borough shopping centers. After attaching the brightly colored laundry ticket to the package, we would place it on the shelf—"The Great Wall of Laundry" to my child's eye.

The biggest difference was that while Gene, Jane, and Vic lassoed their laundry packages with that dreaded burn- and callus-causing rope, Herman and I tidily tied them up with the hand-saving luxury known as tape. For years, the "first generation" reminded the "second generation" of the discrepancy in our laundry duties early and often. Sometimes, all they had to do was show us their hands and the remnants of former calluses and scars in contrast with the clean hands of Herman and me.

As a very young child, during those brief years when The Eng Dynasty still consisted of the seven of us all being present in our laundry, I remember my older siblings' groaning upon the arrival of these deliveries, for it meant we would have a lot of work to do. Later on, as usually the sole child in the laundry, I eagerly awaited the arrival of these boxes and would snatch the papers as soon as the boxes were opened. After the sorting and wrapping work was over, I eagerly filled up sheet after sheet with my pencil portraits. Years later, dramatizing the process and impact of portraiture became a primary focus as a playwright.

The Empress Mother encouraged my drawing and let me do this alongside her break station in the large middle room of our laundry. Repeatedly listening to *Tommy* while alternately gazing at the album cover artwork and drawing my own little pictures completely captivated my nine-year-old psyche and mind—deepening the spell with each playing. But inevitably my reverie would be broken by a bigger power, The Empress Mother's drowning out *Tommy* with what my nine-year-old self called "that dreaded 'Pots and Pans music'"—or what the cultured world calls Cantonese opera. Yes, in the early 1970s, The

Eng Dynasty was probably the only American household in which the kids were pleading with their parents, *"Turn that noise down!"*

In that sacred back room, when not blasting me with shrill morality tales of supernatural Cantonese opera characters, The Empress Mother would frequently lecture me on the ways of the world beyond my little laundry fiefdom: *"Mo ho ngen oh nguy-tie. Um tek ngen. Alloy no ho-gnen oh-key. Mo ho ngen oh nguy-tie."* ["There's no good people out there. They don't feel for people. All the good people you will ever need are right here at home. There are no good people out there."]

For the next thirty years, through the sweeping worldwide changes of the 1970s, 1980s, and 1990s, within the walls of The Eng Dynasty, the song remained the same for the dominating Empress Mother and her obliging Last Emperor of a youngest son. We could have lived in the 1870s . . . or the 1780s . . . or the 1690s.

Over half a century earlier and half a world away, China's actual Last Emperor, Aisin Gioro Pu Yi, was receiving similar information. In 1908, Pu Yi was thrust onto the Emperor's throne at age three to become an unknowing pawn in a ruthless war being waged by his manipulative, self-serving elders. Pu Yi "ruled" for only what would become the final decade of the Qing Dynasty. China's Last Emperor spent most of his life trying to solve the riddle of his birthright and a legacy he was born into but never asked for . . . just like Tommy. For the first quarter-century of Pu Yi's life, that meant his trying to be reinstated as Emperor and returning his family to its former glory. For the first quarter-century of my life, it meant living in constant struggle with my ethnicity as part of my longing to belong.

Chapter 2

Everybody Was Kung Fu Fighting ... or Faking It

IN ADDITION TO being the only Eng Dynasty children to grow up living in a home that was separate from our laundry, Herman and I were also the only ones to grow up with a black-and-white television in in the family area. As only one of our immigrant parents spoke English, let us say that unique interpretations of American television and popular culture of the 1960s and '70s inadvertently ran deep in our family. I remember one particular knock-down/drag-out/take-no-prisoners family screaming match reaching its crescendo with one sibling caterwauling at the other, "You think you're Michael, but you're really Fredo!!!" Yes, in that era it was accepted that the unofficial royal families of America were the Kennedys and the Corleones, and not necessarily in that order.

My name is Alvin, and I am named after that TV chipmunk cartoon character, Alvin from *Alvin and the Chipmunks*. In many ways, it was an affirmative action name bestowed on me by my brother Herman. His affirmative action settlement came not for being named Herman, a fine name, but for the *way* he was named. Yes, it makes much sexier symmetry to say that he was also named after a TV character, a certain Munster patriarch who lived at 1313 Mockingbird Lane. But that show started airing many years after Herman was born. While I grew up thinking, even somehow believing, that he was named after Herman Munster, he was actually named after the eponymous character of the one-panel comic strip "Herman." But it is family fact, not just legend, that Herman and I were the only two of five children whose first names were decided by our siblings and not by our parents . . . sort of.

One family legend is that on the day their yet-unnamed sibling was brought home, wisecracking siblings 1 through 3 had some suggestions.

"He looks like that cartoon," said # 1 son, Gene.

"He does!" seconded first daughter and second child, Jane.

"Yeah, let's call him Herman!" affirmed third child, Vic.

"Ha-ha-ha," all three laughed.

But from the other side of the room they heard The Empress Mother sing a lyrical, *"Herrr-min." "Hor-Mund,"* she sang again with even more melodic authority. The Empress Mother, who didn't speak English, liked how it sounded phonetically. *"Ngooy jung-yee. Ho!"* ["I like it. Good!"], she concluded. The joke was now on wisecracking siblings 1, 2, and 3.

"Mom!" cried Gene.

"You can't name him Herman!" challenged Jane.

"We were just kidding," pleaded Vic.

"Ngooy jung-yee. Ho!" ["I like it. Good!"], The Empress Mother replied emphatically.

Then, everyone looked to Dad.

Dad just stared straight ahead, poker-faced, without saying a word. He took a long, slow drag on his Robert Burns cigarillo, and without making eye contact with anyone in the room, he simply waved his hand as if to say, *whatever your mother wants.* When The Empress Mother put her foot down, the whole family stopped and listened.

Five years later, when I was born, they let Herman name me, and he chose to name me after the lead character of his favorite TV show. To this day I am grateful that his favorite TV shows weren't *Leave It to Beaver* or *Captain Kangaroo.* During my formative years, TV became the definitive cultural barometer bar none. Back then, I didn't see too many three-dimensional Chinese people on that little black-and-white TV in the back room of our laundry. That all started to change in the early 1970s. Or so I thought.

Just as the country was changing in the early '70s, so was television. On the sacred Saturday morning cartoon lineup for us kids, black characters ranging from Fat Albert to The Jackson Five starring as, of course, themselves reigned supreme. In the evenings, race relations, in one way or another, also started to become the prime target of prime-time programming. The show that kickstarted this revolution actually has a tie to Flushing. *All in the Family*, which later spun off the seminal Black prime-time sitcom *The Jeffersons*, is set in Queens. Archie Bunker, the show's controversial protagonist (antagonist?), is even a Flushing High School alum. Flushing High School is on Union Street—three blocks south of our family's laundry. Four of the five Eng siblings attended this high school. Archie Bunker, as brilliantly portrayed by actor Carroll O'Connor, represented the last blue-collar, Eisenhower-era Americana white guy standing in Civil Rights–era–changed (challenged?) Queens and America . . . or so we thought, back then. His battles to haughtily hang on to his old ways became epic comic struggles that made many a person stay home on Saturday, or at least start their Saturday night later, in the early 1970s. Remember, this was well before VCRs, and well, well, well before DVRs and On Demand options.

By the early 1970s, things were also changing on the walls of the bedroom that Herman and I shared. Life-sized black-and-white rock star posters of Jimi Hendrix and The Who's Pete Townshend now vied for attention with a new, full-color poster of all-world martial arts superstar Bruce Lee. That Lee could join this pop culture pantheon was a major statement as Townshend and The Who, in particular, had an enormous influence on Herman and me. Between the Lee and Townshend posters there was also now a nail from which Herman hung his prized nunchucks that he had inscribed with his initials, 'H.E.," on the bottoms of both sticks. (This was several years before nunchucks would be banned in the state of New York from 1974 through 2018 for being lethal weapons!) Bruce Lee had thrust nunchucks into the international spotlight in his groundbreaking films *Enter the Dragon* and *Fists of Fury*. Herman, now a taut, muscular, and ambitious teenager, saw a hero to be emulated in Bruce Lee's cinematic persona—just as he had earlier taken musical inspiration from the adjacent Townshend and Hendrix posters. Clearly, Herman had inherited our immigrant parents' fight and resilience to beat the odds.

On the other side of the bedroom, I was a rotund and laid-back ten-year-old who saw confrontation as something to be avoided at all costs. I had inherited our parents' humbled capacity for retreat, compromise, and, ultimately, the obedient life of a fringe, under-the-radar existence—instilled in them by decades of institutional disenfranchisement. Never as adventurous as Herman, I believed, or at least deeply hoped, that the world would always, somehow, come to me. Instead of taking it to the streets, I stayed home and searched the television for inspiration. I thought I found it in the safe, formulaic martial arts redemption of *Kung Fu*, the TV series starring David Carradine as the Chinese Shaolin priest and martial arts sage Kwai Chang Caine.

As a child in 1972, I wasn't aware of the implications and complications of a Caucasian's playing a Chinese character on television. Of course, I also had no idea that Herman's hero, Bruce Lee, had been humiliatingly passed over for this role. Don't think Herman knew this back then either. I was just thrilled that here, finally, was a Chinese TV character who kicked ass! Was *Kung Fu* cheesy as hell? Hell yeah. But in this landscape of "No C. TV" (no Chinese on television), this Thursday-night show quickly became "Must See TV."

For the first fifty minutes of each episode, Caine was the ultimate pacifist—getting pissed on, spit on, and shit on as he made his journey from the East across America's Wild West in search of his half-brother. But during the show's final ten minutes, watch out! Caine became the precursor to Chow Yun-Fat, Jet Li, and Jackie Chan all rolled into one—kicking any and all Caucasian ass in sight. The whole time, Caine operated under the mantra of "Grasshopper, when you can snatch the pebble from my hand, it will be time for you to leave." This was an incantation from *his* master Shaolin priest, played by the late Keye Luke. I was so enthralled with the show that I even sent away for the Kwai Chang Caine/*Kung Fu* poster that was sold after the conclusion of every episode.

Kung Fu was part of a swelling tide of early 1970s ethnic pride in pop culture that was born of the 1960s' Civil Rights revolution.

But it was the second wave. This tide's first wave included such majestic soul musings as Marvin Gaye's "What's Going On," Curtis Mayfield's "Freddie's Dead," and Stevie Wonder's "Living for the City." These socially conscious hit singles put the plight of urban blight right into the ears, minds, and souls of everyone within hearing distance of a radio. Of course, subsequent waves would be diluted to maintain the status quo mainstream tableaux. This second wave also ushered in the era of "blaxploitation" B- and C-grade films and similar pop culture fare such as the hit single "Everybody Was Kung Fu Fighting." (Remember: *Those cats were fast as lightning—Hoo!! . . . Wha!!!*")

As Herman was starting to make some noise on Queens' rock 'n' roll stages and martial arts studios, I started to pursue my schoolyard dream of being the first Chinese American on the New York Knicks. Remember, this was almost a half-century before Jeremy Lin and "Linsanity." (Do you even remember "Linsanity"?) Between 1970 and 1973, Willis Reed and Walt "Clyde" Frazier led the Knicks on two championship runs in four seasons, lifting us children of the city to hoops heaven. After his historic 1970 Game 7 limp onto the court—despite arthritically injured knees—to inspire the Knicks' first championship, Willis Reed became the embodiment of heroism to an entire generation. Everybody wanted to be Willis Reed . . . except maybe fans of the Los Angeles Lakers, whom the Reed-led Knicks defeated twice in the championship finals. Concurrent with the Knicks' rise to NBA dominance, I became the first and only Chinese player on P.S. 214's first-ever basketball team during the 1972–73 season. In its first year of existence, the P.S. 214 Superstars, a modestly named lot, captured the District 25 title in a showdown with P.S. 209 on the grand stage of the NCAA-sized gymnasium at Queens College.

P.S. 214 Superstars games were played on Friday afternoons. *Kung Fu* was shown on Thursday nights. On Friday mornings, juiced with adrenaline from the previous night's *Kung Fu* episode and jonesing for that afternoon's game, I started imagining that I was . . . Kwai Chang Caine. On the way to school, I started flying around Union Street, landing Kung Fu kicks on unsuspecting classmates. As word spread about my Friday-morning kicking escapades, I soon became the neighborhood's featured kicker in schoolyard and parking lot football games. In those games, my team would go out of their way to kick field goals instead of throwing or running for touchdowns. After a while, I started to believe, or at least fantasize, that I was, like Kwai Chang Caine, the wandering Chinaman with "The Golden Leg." I was sure I was bound for nothing short of righteous truth and kick butt / kick field goal glory.

In class reports, I even started dispensing faux pearls of Chinese wisdom, à la Kwai Chang Caine, such as "the Chinese like to start every day by eating a piece of fruit to show our thanks to the Earth and Sky. . . ." Around Chinese New Year's, I would improvise show-and-tell sessions that were really all show-and-bull. But in my twisted logic, I was slowly achieving what I thought was impossible: I thought I was making being Chinese cool to my classmates on my own terms. But I was only fooling myself.

One morning, breakfast in the back room of our laundry was interrupted as the irate father of one of my classmates burst through the front door. He lunged at the counter and shouted, "If you don't stop kicking my son, I am going to sue you and your whole family." The irate father shook his fist and waved his briefcase for emphasis, turned on his businessman heels, and marched out. Breakfast was over. Dad gave me that stern "Third Strike Look." I first saw that look in the hallways and stairwells of P.S. 214 when Dad came to school to meet with my teacher a few short weeks before . . . when *Kung Fu* first went on the air. My disruptive classroom antics first led to a sentence of an extra homework assignment. A second offense landed me in detention. Strike three was the call home to demand a parent–teacher conference. Dad, being the only English-speaking parent, was subpoenaed to school. Being forced to take time off from the laundry did not put him in a good mood. The day Dad came to school with me was like judgment day. He hated having to take time away from his laundry duties and was completely disappointed by this entire episode. As we walked the two blocks of Union Street, from the laundry to the school, my classmates did not go near or even make eye contact with us. It was an unspoken code of conduct whenever we saw one of our own walking to school with a parent: Dead Child Walking. As we fell into size-place lines in the schoolyard, to file upstairs to our classrooms, Dad first fixed that "Third Strike Look" on me. The look had the same effect as water upon the Wicked Witch of the West . . . "I'm melting!" As the students ascended the stairs on the right side, with teachers and "visiting" adults marching alongside on the left, Dad stopped on every landing to shoot me that stern "Third Strike Look" again.

By the time we reached the third-floor classroom, I had melted into a puddle. But I was a puddle not only because of that "Third Strike Look" but also because of Dad's own look. Wrapped in a ratty, baggy gray-black winter coat and hunter's hat (sort of like a baseball cap with extended beak and earflaps), over his ever-present white shirt, Dad looked every inch the immigrant laundryman. I was deeply embarrassed. Dad's presence made me Chinese on his terms, whereas *Kung Fu*'s Kwai Chang Caine liberated me to at least *think* I was being Chinese on my own terms.

Seeing the "Third Strike Look" at the breakfast table, I knew I was in deep trouble. The Empress Mother quickly cleared the breakfast dishes and went to the front room to sit in Dad's seat behind the front counter—as morning customers started coming in. In the back room, Dad and Herman got their interrogation on.

"If you really want to get into martial arts, kicking the kids at school is not the way to do it," scolded Herman, who was now fifteen and already sounding like the surrogate father he was fast becoming.

Dad just looked on and nodded his head in silent agreement.

"*Kung Fu* is only TV," Herman continued his lecture. "That stuff is all fake."

"So is Bruce Lee!" I lamely counter-chopped.

"Oh no," refuted Dad, finally breaking his stony silence. "Bruce Lee is *real*."

"See!" sneered Herman.

"Caine can fight!" I protested.

"Caine!? . . . He's not even Chinese," bludgeoned Herman.

He took a dramatic pause to let the decisive verbal nunchuck blow sink in.

"David Carradine doesn't know any Kung Fu," started Herman on his victory lap. "They use a stuntman for all the slow-motion fighting at the end of the show. You never see that in a Bruce Lee movie."

Dad nodded affirmatively and lit up one of his ever-present Robert Burns cigarillos, perhaps in celebration of his and Herman's successful nonviolent defensive stand against me. He took a long drag and slowly let out a cloud of smoke. Acknowledging his agreement with Herman, Dad ordered, "Stop making trouble at school."

But all I could hear was, "Grasshopper, when you can snatch the pebble from my hand, it will be time for you to leave."

A few weeks after Herman and Dad's martial arts in media summit, the Kwai Chang Caine poster arrived in the mail. I hung it up on our shared bedroom wall anyway—albeit a re-spectable distance from Herman's "H.E.-inscribed" nunchucks and life-size Hendrix, Townshend, and Bruce Lee posters that occupied the most prominent wall space of the room. Herman and Dad had defeated me into submission, but not into total surrender. I accepted that *Kung Fu* was the fake thing. But it was my fake thing.

Chapter 3

Our Laundry's Roots in Resistance

Family Reunification Along Flushing's Fault Line

IN MANY WAYS, our laundry was a link in the long chain of Chinese American resistance in twentieth-century New York City. In addition to fanning the flames of the fiery Toisan temperament in America, our laundry also grew out of the embers of the Chinese Hand Laundry Alliance. During my formative years, our laundry itself was on the philosophical and physical fault line of a Flushing that was growing ever more divided. While inside the laundry, our family makeup and very name would become forever changed.

In the early twentieth century, nearly a quarter of all Chinese men in America operated a Chinese hand laundry. Just before the Great Depression, there were more than 3,000 single-person-owned and operated Chinese hand laundries in the New York City area alone. Like their West Coast railroad-building and gold-mining forebears of the late nineteenth century, these NYC Chinese laundrymen and women were also being railroaded by racist American trade laws.

The Chinese Hand Laundry Alliance (CHLA) was formed in 1933 in response to a thinly veiled attempt to drive Chinese hand laundrymen and women out of business and out of town— if not out of the country. In 1933, the New York City Board of Aldermen passed a law to limit ownership of laundries to U.S. citizens. The Chinese Consolidated Benevolent Association unsuccessfully challenged this law. From the ashes of this legal defeat rose the CHLA. The CHLA successfully challenged this law, literally saving the livelihoods of what had grown from one-quarter of Chinese men in the NYC area at the turn of the twentieth century to seven-tenths of these men in 1933.

Empowered by this success, one division of the CHLA became a powerful leftist voice of Chinatown—breaking with the status quo Chinatown power structure by aligning themselves with Mao Zedong's Chinese Communist Party (CCP) and organizing several "Save China" campaigns. This stance grew out of their opposition to both the 1930s Japanese invasion of Manchuria and subsequent occupation of China, and the enabling non-resistance put up by China's then-ruling Kuomintang party (KMT), led by Chiang Kai-Shek. Mao's CCP would eventually defeat the KMT, forcing its members to flee China—leading to the founding of Taiwan. But the KMT would retain primary political control of New York's Chinatown for the rest of the twentieth century.

In one of their most brazen displays of power, in 1938 the pro-Mao faction of the CHLA raised money to purchase an ambulance, loaded it with medical supplies, and shipped it off to China as a gift for Mao. The ambulance doors were emblazoned with the dedication "For the Heroic Defenders of China from the Chinese Hand Laundry Alliance, New York."

The CHLA instantly became a lightning rod for Wisconsin Senator Joseph McCarthy's "Red Scare" Communist interrogations in the 1940s. This Red Scare campaign resulted in the high-profile House Un-American Activities Committee (HUAC) hearings in the 1950s. This intense, often extreme surveillance greatly reduced the ranks of CHLA membership to the point where it nearly folded. While the CHLA outlived McCarthyism and still exists today—albeit in a very changed role—the damage was done.

Dad and The Empress Mother opened their first Foo J. Chin Chinese Hand Laundry during the height of this HUAC hysteria—just across the Hudson River from New York City's Chinatown, in Hoboken, New Jersey, in 1946. Even though Senator McCarthy was censured by the Senate in December 1954, my parents would spend the rest of their professional and personal hours haunted by the ghost of McCarthy's Red Scare tactics.

My older siblings and cousins recall my parents' hosting dinners, barbecues, and parties with relatives and neighboring Toisan hand laundry families. For these occasions, Dad even acted as the M.C.—dressing like Frank Sinatra, playing Ol' Blue Eyes' music on the stereo, cracking jokes, and basically being the life of the party. Sadly, I never knew those parents. In contrast with my siblings and cousins' recollections, I feel as if I had half-parents.

By the time I was growing up, Dad and The Empress Mother had already been through raising four kids and nearly two decades of living in virtual exile in disenfranchised immigrant America. They were tired. Tired of fighting with each other. Tired of fighting with their children. Tired of fighting the American way. I cannot recall even one event like the dinners, barbecues, and parties that my older siblings and cousins remember attending. Of course, there were formal banquets in Chinatown for weddings and "Red Eggs"—a.k.a. one-year birthday celebrations of grandchildren—but there were never any parties or celebrating at home. As a child who had not yet learned about McCarthyism and its impact on my parents and all of their relatives and relations from their generation, I interpreted this isolated lifestyle as being above it all. Much later on, I would realize that my parents' "under-the-radar" existence was a result of decades of personal and institutionalized antagonism. Even when they had a more active social life, they never even considered socializing or networking beyond their established, and therefore safe, NYC–Toisan Chinese hand laundry circles.

By the late 1960s, Flushing, like most of the country and the world, had become a divided land. Most of my Jewish friends lived west of Union Street in the more "urban district" comprising primarily apartment buildings. Most of my Gentile friends lived east of Union Street in the more "suburban district" among a consortium of private homes built as part of the post–World War II housing boom in the 1950s. Beyond the farthest western edge of the "urban district" lay "the projects"—New York City Housing Authority (NYCHA) apartment building complexes where most of Flushing's black and Latin population lived. Sadly, in the segregated ways that ruled the world that was my Flushing childhood, these three districts rarely intersected or even interacted . . . except on the basketball court. There and then the only thing that mattered was the quality and tenacity of your game. Yet after the games—whether they were schoolyard pick-up games or, later, school-organized league games—we all went back to our separate districts.

As fate would have it, the Flushing edition of the Foo J. Chin Chinese Hand Laundry was right *on* Union Street—Flushing's unofficial DMZ between the "suburban Gentile" and "urban Jewish" districts. Though only a few blocks separated the quote unquote "suburban Gentile" and "urban Jewish" districts, they were like two different worlds . . . and I constantly shuttled between them. We used the laundry's address as our home address. As the laundry was on the "urban Jewish" west side of the dividing line that was Union Street, I attended P.S. 214, the public grade school of that "district." But most days after school, I hung around with the Gentile guys who lived on the block where The First Flushing Palace was located . . . until we would have one of our frequent childhood fallouts. Then I'd hang out exclusively with my friends in the urban Jewish section and vice versa. To paraphrase the late, great "Man in Black," Johnny Cash, "I walked the line" between the Jewish and Gentile communities of our neighborhood. For me, this came to a head in the eighth grade. During the week, I watched with envy as many of my Catholic classmates left school early to attend religious instruction in preparation for their First Communion. On the weekends, I must have spent every other Saturday dancing the Hora at a classmate's Bar or Bat Mitzvah.

While I never felt like a complete outsider, part of me always felt that I could be a *paisan* only to a certain point with my Gentile friends, and I could be a *mensch* to only a certain point with my Jewish friends. This was the "small town" part of growing up in Flushing. The "big city" part of growing up in Flushing was adapting and learning to use this divide to create your own space for psychological survival—rather than being held captive by one group of friends and their expectations and demands. So, in the big city you could be as visible or as invisible as you liked.

My parents were really good at this. Everybody in the neighborhood knew them, but they didn't know anybody. It didn't help that even though we lived only three blocks from our laundry, my parents climbed aboard their old gray Oldsmobile to drive to and from our laundry every day. You're not going to meet a lot of the neighbors that way! But they fought long and hard for their piece of the American pie and they were going to savor every last crumb . . . even if it meant driving their huge, gas-guzzling four-door for the three blocks to and from the laundry every day at 7:00 A.M. and 7:00 P.M., six days a week, fifty-two weeks of most years.

Perhaps through the suburban influence of finally having a private home that was separate from our laundry, and with it a larger kitchen than the cramped "urban tenement frontier family" stove and sink in our laundry's back room, the sacred family dinner started showing signs of culinary encroachment from the outside Western world. Around this time, my parents had been together in the United States for more than twenty-five years and were finally, if reluctantly, acknowledging American cuisine. We started eating "exotic" American delicacies, such as sandwiches! The sandwiches were served alongside our standard staple of every meal: mounds and mounds of rice . . . or corned beef, cabbage, and potatoes, accompanied by mounds and mounds of rice. Hamburgers, french fries, and . . . you know what. Around this time, in the back room of our laundry where we took all of our meals during the week, "extra starch" was not reserved just for shirt collars anymore.

The cramped workweek kitchen of our laundry's back room was the domain of The Empress Mother from Monday to Saturday afternoons. Dad would take over the cooking on Saturday nights in the back room, and on Sundays and all holidays in the larger semi-suburban kitchen of The First Flushing Palace. For most Saturday-night dinners, to wind down from an exhausting twelve-hours-a-day six-day work week, Dad, a big-time carnivore, would cook up a big steak or similar red meat entrée. With this came our beloved *"Ligh-Pie-Loook Fon"*—my phonetics for "Saturday-night rice." For these special Saturday-night dinners, our "mounds and mounds of rice" would get drizzled or deluged—depending on one's taste—with gravy from our meat entrée.

Dad's carnivorous desires led him to also start cooking up huge pots of spaghetti and meatballs. Over time, he would become obsessed with making those meatballs—blending meats, making his own breadcrumbs, finding the finest parsley. The Empress Mother still insisted on taking rice with her spaghetti and meatballs, but Herman and I were, eventually, excused from this ritual.

On holidays such as Thanksgiving, both Dad and The Empress Mother would create hybrid East–West feasts featuring turkey and most of the American standards supplemented with Chinese rice noodles, Cantonese-styled lobster and spare ribs . . . alongside mounds and mounds of rice. Of course, Chinese or Lunar New Year feasts were off the charts with . . . everything! . . . And the mounds and mounds of rice never had any Western intervention on the Lunar New Year table.

My family's "domestic journey to the East"—this one taking them from Hoboken, New Jersey, to Flushing, Queens—also took them straight into the heart of the 1960s' "New Frontier" and "Great Society" administrations of Democratic presidents John F. Kennedy and Lyndon B. Johnson. These administrations created the landmark 1965 Immigration and Nationality Act—a watershed moment for Chinese and Asian families in America.

Before 1965, more than 90 percent of U.S. immigration quotas were designated for northern and western European countries. The Immigration and Nationality Act of 1965 leveled the playing field by instituting the same flat quota of 20,000 immigrants for every country outside of the Western Hemisphere. A second provision of this act placed a priority on re-uniting the families of immigrants in America in what is now maligned as "chain immigration."

Dad saw these 1965 changes in immigration policy as an opportunity to bring his Mom to the United States. In order to achieve this, he had to change his "paper name" of Chin back to his ancestral Eng—paper names being those that were on illegally purchased documents that my father and many Chinese immigrants had to procure in order to circumvent the Chinese Exclusion Act—the first and hopefully last U.S. law that made it illegal for one group of people to become American citizens. I remember Herman's telling me of the confusion this created for him at P.S. 214. Understanding it must have been a herculean task for an eight-year old. Thankfully, I was only three and unaware of the entire episode. At least consciously.

Having the same last name as his mother bolstered Dad's case to bring her over following the passage of the Immigration and Nationality Act of 1965 and its emphasis on family reunification. A generous contribution to a local assemblyman's re-election campaign pork-barreled Grandma's immigration case protected by the subterfuge of a numerous series of bills being passed by this assemblyman. The formerly Foo J. Chin Chinese Hand Laundry family was now legally the Eng family.

Dad's Mom finally arrived in 1966, at the recently renamed John F. Kennedy International Airport in Jamaica, Queens. In 1966, going to the airport was still a special occasion that people got dressed up for. In this spirit, the newly renamed Eng Dynasty all put on their Sunday best—outfits usually worn to promenade proudly around Chinatown—and went *en masse* to meet Dad's Mom at JFK airport. A tense air of anticipation and mystery filled their lungs and minds, as well as the silence that surrounded the family.

Finally, Dad's Mom appeared, a poor but proudly dressed Toisan countrywoman amidst a sea of Chinese humanity. That occasion was the only time my brother Herman ever recalls seeing Dad cry. The Empress Mother was not nearly as moved by the arrival of her arranged husband's biological mother.

The arrival of Dad's Mom lit a different kind of flame under Dad. During the year following her arrival, he became eager to expand his base in America to show his Mom how far he had come. The Empress Mother often talked about how Dad wanted to invest in stocks, but she insisted on real estate as she fashioned herself a "business-y lady." Thus, the Eng Dynasty acquired a second property to supplement The First Flushing Palace. The new acquisition was a semi-detached three-family unit on the urban Jewish west side of Union Street. This second property became The Dynasty's rental outpost.

Tending to this second property became a chore that only Herman and I had to endure, as its acquisition concurred with the first generation of Eng siblings' going off to college . . . although all siblings, except for Jane, would later live in this property. About once a month, Herman and I assisted Dad on his maintenance rounds of the rental units in the three-family dwelling.

Within the walls of The First Flushing Palace and on walks around our block, Dad's Mom became a curiosity. An even more pronounced Chinese presence than The Empress Mother, this petite, androgynous-looking woman, often dressed in robes or long dresses, strolled around in silence offering only her enigmatic smile that featured at least one prominent gold tooth. If the outer boroughs' "suburban Gentile" neighbors on our block regarded The Empress Mother as an alien because she did not speak English, who knows what they thought of her mother-in-law from an arranged marriage.

There was immediate tension between Grandmother Eng and The Empress Mother—the former Toy Lain Chin. With every breath and step, Dad's Mom was eroding the autonomy that The Empress Mother had crossed oceans, cultures and continents to earn. Somewhere, deep inside, The Empress Mother also had to be burning with a primal rage at being abandoned by *her* Mom.

When she was eight, the father of The Empress Mother died from untended medical complications caused by a lack of supplies during the Japanese occupation of China. In the wake of his death, The Empress Mother's Mom fled their Toisan village, leaving both the eight-year-old Empress Mother and her younger brother, Hong On Wong, to be raised by village elders. On his own separate emigration journey from Toisan to America, the Empress Mother's brother would eventually settle in New York's Chinatown, marry, and raise a family of six wonderful sons: Steven, Stanley, Chester, Eddie, Bill/"Boo," and Ning Wong.

Dad's Mom lived in The First Flushing Palace for only a very brief few years. Adult complications far beyond my childhood ken resulted in Dad's Mom's fleeing Flushing to live with other relatives and Toisan village friends in the Oakland, California, area. She remained estranged from her son and everyone else in The Eng Dynasty for the rest of her life for reasons that are still unclear to me. The morning that Dad's Mom died was one of the most turbulent days in the thirty-year history of the Foo J. Chin Chinese Hand Laundry.

"*Koy awe ngan, koy awe see-fee, koy-yigh!*" ["All this money, all of this nasty tension, what a waste!"] blasted The Empress Mother at the beginning of an epic ten-minute Toisan takedown. She was going ballistic on Dad—feeling that The Eng Dynasty squandered too much money, time, and good will in bringing Grandmother Eng to America.

Dad did not respond. He just sat in silence, staring past The Empress Mother and out into space. A vast space that was his isolation in his adopted country. A country that never completely accepted him. It was here in the U.S.A. that Dad reunited with his mother only to become estranged from her a second time. Something must have told him that this second separation would be their final one. Throughout The Empress Mother's tirade, Dad never stopped sorting the dirty laundry that lay all around his feet.

Chapter 4

:::

It's Only a Paper Son

The Chinatown Bachelor Society

AS A CHILD I never gave the name of our laundry, Foo J. Chin, a second thought. Now, as an adult, I find it a source of endless fascination. In all of the black-and-white photographs that document Dad and The Empress Mother's thirty years of being Chinese hand laundry proprietors, Foo J. Chin looms like a ghost or a silent witness. Hovering just over the heads of everyone in the picture frame, the name Foo J. Chin is on every wooden shingle and neon sign that announced to the world, "The Eng Dynasty is open for business."

Like so many Chinese of his generation, Dad entered America in the 1930s as an illegal "paper son." This means he had purchased false identification papers. Foo J. Chin was the name on his purchased papers. Dad had to immigrate this way in order to evade the United States' Chinese Exclusion Act. Passed in 1882, the Chinese Exclusion Act not only barred Chinese from immigrating to the United States, but it also forbade legal Chinese residents from becoming citizens, marrying other citizens, or bringing their wives over. Of course, a few exceptions could always be made for prominent merchants, diplomats, and students. At the height of this act, the male-to-female ratio in most American Chinatowns was over twenty men to one woman. This law came to be regarded not as the Chinese Exclusion Act, but as "The Chinese Extinction Act." The law was finally repealed in 1943, when the United States found it advantageous to have an alliance with China during World War II.

■■■

Use of this "paper son" practice rose in proportion to the Chinese Exclusion Act's enforcement. This rise was exponentially aided by the occidental maxim that "all Chinese look alike" and further abetted by the 1906 San Francisco earthquake. That natural disaster destroyed most of the official records of the city that had the largest Chinese population in America. In the pre–computer/digital data era, Chinese identities were for several decades virtually impossible to trace accurately. This situation opened a wider window of opportunity for Chinese immigrants to climb through and take a walk on the wild side in "the good ol' U.S. of A."

After Dad entered America illegally as Foo J. Chin in the 1930s, he started working in restaurants in New York City's Chinatown. Through his restaurant work, Dad became, by Toisan village standards, a rich man. In 1934, as the conflicts were beginning to erupt that would eventually explode into the full-fledged Second Sino-Japanese War, he went back to China as "big man in village"—so to speak. A marriage was arranged to The Empress Mother, who was all of fourteen years young. Dad was a much more mature sixteen. After their arranged marriage, Dad went back to New York. The Empress Mother did not see or hear from him for ten years. So, let's just think about this: A boy born in a piss-poor village in China is now a young man in New York City with more money in his pocket than he ever imagined. . . . I don't think he spent those ten years feathering the nest for The Empress Mother's arrival.

Every Sunday of my childhood, we would venture across two bridges and three boroughs, from Flushing, Queens, across Brooklyn and over the Manhattan Bridge to Chinatown. These weekly ventures also gave me subliminal glimpses into the very different, almost polar opposite dispositions of Dad and The Empress Mother. It was literally like night and day.

During the day, we would visit The Empress Mother's Chinatown of family, friends, dim sum, and shopping. When the sun went down, we were in Dad's Chinatown. Namely, in the balcony of that rundown, old Chinatown movie house The Rosemary Theatre. While my parents would be captivated by the on-screen larger-than-life Cantonese opera and melodrama performers in what my eight-year-old self categorized as "Pots and Pans Movies," I would be captivated and even a little leery of all of the old men sitting by themselves—bathed in the half-light of the often violent imagery of Cantonese cinema.

In the evening, Chinatown's loud, bustling, family-filled streets gave way to a quiet, desolate, and dirty cityscape that seemed to be populated solely by individual members of the fabled "Chinatown Bachelor Society."

The Chinatown Bachelor Society men were the living legacy or walking wounded of America's Chinese Exclusion Act. The laws and the tide turned too late for these men. Their prime years, when they could have married or brought over wives and established families, were long gone. Now their world was that netherworld known as Chinatown at night. They came out only after the tourists left and the shops shut down. This generation carried the historical weight and psychological scars of being the isolated sons of the men who built the transcontinental railroad and then were not invited to take part in the celebration and historical photo commemorating its completion. Most of these isolated men lived many years of sporadic outsider work and sporadic outsider pay. Decades of tough breaks, tough love, or little to no love shaped these men's outlooks, insights, even their body language. Individually, they appeared ill at ease, even perplexed that they somehow wound up living alone in New York City's Lower Manhattan circa late-twentieth-century America. But with one another, they seemed to create and complete a seamless, timeless world of their own—one you could feel but never touch.

Looking back, it makes perfect sense that every Sunday night at The Rosemary Theatre, Dad would carry on with these isolated Chinatown Bachelor Society men with greater grace and ease than he did in any other stratum of his life. Dad may have had five biological children and an arranged wife of his own. But spiritually, he would always be a member of the Chinatown Bachelor Society.

Chapter 5

▞▞

Addressees

WHEN I WAS old enough to start wanting to abandon my laundry duties to go out and play with my friends, The Empress Mother was very tolerant of my adolescent restlessness. But this did not sit well at all with Dad.

"The way you're always running out of here," Dad would scold with exasperation, "you'd think this place was full of ghosts!"

We just stared at each other in silence. In that silence, the front room of the laundry seemed to fill up with the spirits of all the Chinese hand laundrymen and women who had come before us, as well as the relatives and friends who no longer came to visit. The laundry's ether was already thick with an abundance of Cantonese opera supernatural spirits—whether or not my parents were blasting their records. After a beat or two that seemed like an eternity, The Empress Mother would inevitably break the standoff by saying, *"Ee Ka-woy Fahn!"* ["Let him go play!"] And off I would run to the basketball courts of the P.S. 214 schoolyard or wherever my friends were gathering.

As in most dynamics between a mother and her youngest child, The Empress Mother was always bailing me out and letting me off the hook. The tenderness and generosity The Empress Mother shared with me was a tiny island in the increasingly stormy sea of hostilities that was becoming her daily journey with my Dad. The emotional undertow from this ocean of constant confrontations would soon start pulling me down in every still or idle moment—particularly when I was alone. In these moments, it was all I could do to keep from drowning in waves of profound sadness, distance, and isolation that were continually crashing my psyche. This emotional albatross even informed how I would interpret innocent 1970s pop song lyrics on the radio. When The Eagles sang, "So often times it happens that we live our lives in chains and we never even know we had the key," or when Bachman-Turner Overdrive sang, "Girl, my life is not complete, I've never seen you smile," all I could think was this is how my parents must feel every second of every day.

Luckily, we all had our respites from this daily drudgery. Mine came on the basketball court and in the schoolyard. On Sundays in Chinatown, Dad had his nighttime exchanges with his Chinatown Bachelor Society cronies and The Empress Mother had her afternoon dim sum and shopping walk-and-talks with family and friends. She also had the additional joyous ritual of writing to and receiving letters from fellow Toisan pen pals—primarily the Woo family of Oakland, California, and the Chew family of Chicago, Illinois. Over time I would come to truly understand the meaning and significance behind The Empress Mother's connection to these two families.

My part of this letter-writing correspondence always gave me great joy.

"Addressee!" The Empress Mother would lovingly command upon the completion of her latest Chinese calligraphy–crafted missive to be mailed out to the West Coast or the Midwest.

"*Gnooy loy luh*" ["I'm on the way"], I responded and sprinted into action.

My addressee routine started with first fishing out her addressee book—a handwritten list of The Empress Mother's Chinese characters alongside my CAPITAL ENGLISH LETTERS from beneath a pile of notes, Chinese newspapers, and the odd abacus that had accumulated in and around her station of the laundry. As The Empress Mother was also a writer of copious memos and rhymed expressions, this pile got to be quite high some weeks. On those pages, she often couched many life lessons in rhymes such as "*Pock pock see-you, ho pong yu.*" ["Clap hands, make good friends."] This bilingual addressee book was hand-scrawled on the brown cardboard back of a previous year's promotional calendar from a Chinatown grocer or merchant. In retrospect, the writing and editing of this list was one of the few things, if not the only thing, that The Empress Mother, Dad, and I ever collaborated on. Dad was the go-between in translating The Empress Mother's Toisan Cantonese for accuracy, and I was the scribe and analog–human being spellcheck—which often broke down to phonetic spellings of Toisan names and notes.

After fishing out this precious addressee book from the piles of The Empress Mother's notes, I addressed the envelopes for my mother's handwritten Chinese letters and mailed them. Then, after responses arrived, I happily sorted them out for her. Remembering the joy in The Empress Mother's face as she wrote and read those letters still makes me smile. Our addressee ritual reached its apex when the Woo family announced that they wanted to come to New York from Oakland to visit. The Empress Mother was elated. Even my Dad was excited that they wanted to visit. While the Chew family from Chicago had visited us here in New York City several times, this would be the Woo family's first visit to New York.

"Addressee!" paged The Empress Mother after reading the Woo family's news.

"*Gnooy loy luh*" ["I'm on the way"], I confirmed and dutifully fished out the addressee book as I had so many times before. Only this time, when I handed it to her, she looked up the phone number and picked up the laundry telephone instead of a letter envelope. With assistance from Dad, The Empress Mother dialed all ten digits (dialing 1 was not yet required) and called all the way to the other side of the country. That was one of the first times I saw both parents agree to make a then-costly long-distance call—all the way to California! When the actual addressees, Mrs. Chun Oy Woo and Mr. Art Ming Woo, finally arrived in human form, my parents became a pair of joyful, dutiful tour guides! I vividly recall tagging along for one memorable day in Manhattan when we visited the United Nations, went up to the observation deck of the Empire State Building, and then drove down to Chinatown for a banquet-sized dinner. Back then, the Woos were "just" the addressees from Oakland. Now, I fully comprehend who they were in the emotional and tangible life of The Empress Mother.

At a very young age, The Empress Mother and her brother, Hong On Wong, became orphans following the passing of their father and subsequent abandonment by their mother. That was when village elders Chun Oy Woo and Art Ming Woo stepped up to become their *de facto* parents. How The Empress Mother immigrated to America revolves around Roy T. Chew—whose family she regularly wrote to in Chicago.

In 1946, ten years after my parents' arranged marriage and three years after The Chinese Exclusion Act was repealed, The Empress Mother made her voyage to the United States. She arrived not as the proud wife of my Dad but as the "paper wife" of Roy T. Chew. Though it had been ten years since The Empress Mother had seen her husband, with the vital assistance of Mr. Chew she was now coming to America to straighten Dad's ass out! Even now, in our twenty-first-century heads, it's hard to fathom that The Empress Mother journeyed to the other side of the planet, to a country where she didn't speak the language or know the culture, to link her life to someone who legally was her husband but was really a stranger.

During my childhood years, the Chew family stayed in contact with ours—regularly driving from Chicago to stay with us here in NYC for several days. Back then, I could not fully grasp Roy's significance to our family. Years later, after he retired to southern California, I was lucky to have the opportunity to meet up with him again in person at a family banquet in the L.A. area. Between courses, I asked him how and why he helped The Empress Mother immigrate to America.

"Roy, if you don't mind me asking, did you help bring my mother into this country as a financial arrangement? And it's fine if it was."

"No. It was not a financial arrangement," recalled Roy. "I was an American citizen and a veteran. I was able to help reunite several Chinese families . . . can I finish dinner now?"

With tears of gratitude in my eyes I mouthed "Yes," and Roy most deservedly dove back into the noodles, fish, and veggies piled high on his banquet plate by his wife and grandchildren. I feasted on the moment.

The Chew and Woo family visits were among the few times that I remember both of my parents' being genuinely happy and seeming to enjoy each other's company. The importance of both of these families to The Empress Mother were enough for even my warring parents to maintain a truce during their visits—giving big face to all addressees and addresser.

Without these Oakland and Chicago addressees, The Empress Mother might never have survived her tumultuous childhood, questionable start to her arranged marriage, and, ultimately, immigration to America. It will always take a village, as well as a few addressees.

Chapter 6

▋▋▋

Disappearing Acts

That Old-Time Religion

"DAD! DAD! IS she ever gonna come back?" I cried.

"Don't worry, son," offered Dad, without making eye contact. "She'll be back. A bad penny always comes back."

As my parents' violent arguments started erupting more and more frequently, The Empress Mother started periodically fleeing our laundry and family. The first such "disappearing act" took place on a winter weeknight. Business was slow, so it was just me and Dad in an eerily quiet laundry. As I sat paralyzed—unable to even attempt my homework—Dad started drilling something. After a few minutes, he completed his project and shared it with me. With a bizarre grin on his face, he held up a coin, a quarter with a hole he had just drilled straight through George Washington's head. He then slid the pierced coin onto his keychain—right next to his car keys.

"This way," Dad explained, "when I die at least I'll have two-bits on me."

I had no response.

"Come on, let's go get something to eat," announced Dad, and closed the laundry early that night. This was previously unheard of.

We climbed aboard the family's new 1972 *Titanic*-sized navy blue Chrysler Newport and Dad started the engine—the new pierced quarter on his keychain conspicuously luminous in the dashboard glow. He drove us downtown and found a spot in Flushing's gunmetal-gray municipal parking lot near Main Street.

"I'm gonna make a quick stop at O.T.B. [Off-Track Betting]," decided Dad.

"Da-ad. Can you . . . not bet too much?" I pleaded.

"Don't worry, kid. Just wait here," Dad said before disappearing into the smoky O.T.B.—leaving his ten-year-old alone in the parking lot.

Dinner that night was a nondescript takeout meal eaten with plastic forks and knives off of styrofoam paper plates in the barren-feeling First Flushing Palace. For dessert, Dad got into some serious scotch drinking.

"Are you gonna be all right?" I asked Dad without looking at him—fearful of any eye contact. This time, Dad had no response.

Just as The Empress Mother had fled the laundry to seek sanctuary from Dad's violence, I was terrified of facing the same fate. I was fearful that the situation and the scotch might provoke Dad into using the same physical discipline he had used to govern his other four children and his wife. His physical discipline was most intense with his #1 son, Gene. The firstborn usually has it the toughest—being that the parents are, of course, newbies to parenting. For The Empress Mother and Dad, this newness to parenting was exacerbated by their being illegal immigrants who had just escaped a brutal Japanese occupation and an unforgiving civil war in China. Many of these pressures were transferred onto Gene's young shoulders.

Over the years, these pressures often drove Dad to physically discipline my older siblings. Sometimes it would be a simple slap to keep them in line. Other times it was a flat-out beating. Gene grew up to become a teetotaling ROTC-trained taskmaster and a devout Lutheran. This was in direct opposition to Dad's hard drinking, at times reckless ways, as well as his being a nonpracticing Catholic by virtue of his having accepted shelter and resettling assistance but not religious relief from Jesuit missionaries at different points in his life.

Around this time, Gene got the family involved with True Light Lutheran Church in Chinatown. True Light is the powerful yet inviting regal building that wraps around the northeast corner of Worth and Mulberry streets—just up the hill from the infamous former "Five Corners" that is now Columbus Park. With its arching stained-glass windows and rescue mission–like neon cross adorning its Worth Street entrance, True Light has beamed like a beacon since 1948. Gene attended True Light faithfully and as one of its most active and respected congregation members, even delivering some guest sermons. He set an example that The Empress Mother and I wanted to follow.

"Uh, Mom, Dad?" I shyly summoned an impromptu Eng Dynasty politburo over breakfast one morning. "Since we go to Chinatown every Sunday, why don't we also start going to True Light? . . . Just like Gene."

"Nah," immediately vetoed Dad, moving to crush my motion.

"*Gnooy jung-yee hoe.*" ["Good, I like that,"] countered The Empress Mother, eager to expand her Chinatown interests.

"I'll drop you off," conceded Dad.

It was not quite a second coming of the Flushing Remonstrance—in which Quakers mounted a successful rebellion against the colonizing British for the first uprising for religious freedom in America. But as The Empress Mother and I eagerly joined "Gene's Remonstrance," dropping us off at the curb was about as close as Dad wanted to get to True Light.

For an early-1970s rock and pop culture–obsessed ten-year-old, such a church experiment was not as great a leap as it sounds. Pop culture was filled with spirituality, or at least a yearning to fill that existential void in each of us. Even progressive-rock FM radio stations regularly played a variety of hip hymns ranging from Blind Faith's "Presence of the Lord" to The Doobie Brothers' "Jesus Is Just Alright with Me." Ex-Beatle George Harrison's "My Sweet Lord" remained a staple on both FM progressive-rock and AM Top 40 radio stations—inspiring his enormous legion of post-Beatles listeners to strive for those twin spires of rock 'n' roll and religious transcendence. If The Who's *Tommy* was my first rock 'n' roll experience, then "My Sweet Lord" and Harrison's concert film of *The Concert for Bangladesh* were my first religious rock 'n' roll experiences.

Moreover, as George Harrison was the youngest Beatle and always considered the "little brother" of the band, I immediately felt a strong bond with him.

Seeing the *Concert for Bangladesh* film was also one of the first journeys that Herman and I made to "The City," or what we '70s outer borough kids will always call Manhattan, by ourselves without Dad and The Empress Mother. We rode the #7 train for its entire route—at that time, from Main Street, Flushing, all the way to Times Square. The now Disneyfied family-friendly "crossroads of the world" was back then in the declining final decade of its long run as the definitive sin center of America, if not of the world. And it was still very much open for adult business. Walking from the 7 train's last stop in Manhattan, through Times Square and its colorful assortment of shady and dangerous-looking characters, I was thankful to be under the protective guidance of my fifteen-year-old brother. By this time, Herman had already been through this rite of passage of fighting off NYC's unnatural elements in the name of scoring a hardcore rock 'n' roll fan fix.

The year before, Herman scored his first fan fix by sleeping out all night outside of Shea Stadium to "cop" tickets to see Grand Funk Railroad become the first group since The Beatles to rock Flushing's first baseball/rock 'n' roll citadel (long before it would be demolished to make room for Citibank Field). His overnight foray to get tickets earned him a sound beating from Dad when he tried to tiptoe back into the house. But judging from the glow on Herman's face after the concert, the punishment was nothing compared with the pleasure.

Now Herman was taking his little brother to the cavernous DeMille Theater in the heart of Times Square. Yes, it was only a rock concert on film and not in the flesh, but the flick did the trick. I entered Times Square an innocent child and left there a boy addicted—painfully pining for my next hardcore rock 'n' roll fan fix and unable to think much about anything else.

■■■

Sunday services at True Light are in English at 10:30 A.M. and in Cantonese at 12:30 P.M. Since I didn't speak Cantonese and The Empress Mother spoke very little English, we had to alternate between the two services. We began our church experiment with an English-language service on a weekend in which Gene was out of town. The Empress Mother and I dutifully made our way to the front pew, saying hello to all of Gene's friends along the way.

"Gene Quong, *my* son," The Empress Mother introduced herself in halting English—claiming her royalty.

"Uh . . . and I'm Gene's little brother," I nervously announced in the way that one flails just before drowning.

As soon as we sat down, The Empress Mother picked up a bilingual Chinese–English Bible and began a private study session.

"Please rise," intoned Pastor Yang.

The longtime True Light pastor's amplified Cantonese-inflected English reverberated around the canyon-like nave. A *whoosh* of shuffling Sunday-best clothing filled the air, underscored by the creak of wooden pews' being relieved of human weight. The congregation rose . . . save for one.

"*Khee!*" ["Stand!"] I pleaded to The Empress Mother.

"*Koy-see?*" ["Now?"] she asked.

"Yes!" I implored.

The Empress Mother majestically rose to her full, 4′10″ height.

"Please be seated," offered Pastor Yang.

Then the vicar, a young Caucasian man from the Midwest, ascended the pulpit to deliver that morning's sermon. The vicar was a friend of Gene's who was always trying to get me to enroll in Sunday school and work toward confirmation. The Empress Mother returned to her Bible study—turning page after page— as we sat in the front pew, directly in front of the vicar.

I tried to stay with the vicar's sermon, but my mind and eyes kept wandering to the beatific mural of blue sky and clouds above True Light's altar. I started to contemplate the significance of the clouds and blue sky and also tried to comprehend how many True Light parishioners would ponder this same question, while distracted from a sermon, before and after this moment. After a while, I started to meditate on the mural and on Jesus's face on a nearby statue. The more I meditated, Jesus's white robe morphed into a white suit. From the pocket of that white suit, He produced a white Stratocaster electric guitar. Behind Him, Ringo Starr appeared on drums . . . to His left appeared Eric Clapton on lead guitar . . . Angels descended from the mural's blue sky and clouds chanting, "Hallelujah! Hare Krishna!" Jesus had transformed into George Harrison at *The Concert for Bangladesh*—"My Sweet Lord"! George then stepped up to the mic and announced, "Let us now take communion."

The vicar had concluded his sermon—breaking my rock-and-religion fantasy. The vicar descended the pulpit and started installing the modular rail for that month's communion ritual. I was the first in line. *Just like Gene*, I thought to myself.

As I got down on my knees to kneel and receive, the vicar made eye contact with me, leaned down, and whispered: "Communion is only for people who have achieved confirmation."

The vicar then politely offered the bread (a.k.a. "The Body of Christ"), but not the wine (a.k.a. "The Blood of Christ"). I returned to my seat accepting this bloodless tie to True Light.

Thankfully, The Empress Mother was still deep into her private Chinese Bible study and hadn't even noticed what had happened.

▟▟

"Let us pray," invoked Pastor Yang, resuming the running of the church service from the visiting vicar.

The entire congregation, this time including The Empress Mother, rose as one.

Pastor Yang led the parishioners in reciting "The Lord's Prayer"—the English-speaking parishioners, that is. A period of silent prayer followed.

"Dear Lord: Sorry I messed up, but I'll do better next week. . . . Please help me make the P.S. 214 basketball team; and please, please, please help the Knicks in the playoffs. Willis is out for the season and the Celtics and Bullets look really tough . . . ." Then, somewhere outside of my silent prayer reverie, I felt a nudge.

"*Taw!*" ["Sit down!"] urged The Empress Mother.

I opened my eyes to see Pastor Yang staring straight down at me. Silent Prayer time was over, and he was waiting for me to sit down.

"*Ai-Yah*," ["Oh, God"] groaned The Empress Mother with embarrassment.

That first day turned out to be the beginning of the end of this church experiment for me. I soon reached my teenage years and was relieved of taking part in my parents' weekly Sunday sojourns to Chinatown. But The Empress Mother became a regular member of the congregation. Dad continued to drop her off, still preferring to stay a sidewalk's width away from True Light.

One of the two times I remember Dad's actually entering True Light was in August 1970, when Gene got married there. Gene's wedding was followed in quick succession by Vic's in November, a few blocks away from True Light at Chinatown's Transfiguration Catholic Church, and Jane's in December—many miles away near the Canadian border with upstate New York. Within the span of five months, the "first generation" of The Eng Dynasty had all gotten married. Gene and Vic married Chinese spouses, resulting in what, from a Toisan/Flushing perspective, could be interpreted as mixed marriages. But there was no denying that Jane was entering a bona fide mixed marriage. There was also no denying its impact. For Old World Chinese families like ours, when one of their children breaks the circle by marrying a non-Chinese, that wedding day becomes "a day that will live in infamy." But in many ways, Gene's marriage to Frances Teng crossed even more cultural lines than Jane's.

Gene married into a sophisticated, Mandarin-speaking northern Chinese family from "The City." The Tengs were cosmopolitan doctors and intellectuals of Manhattan's Upper East Side and Shanghai, while the Engs were working- and farmer-class salts of the Earth from Flushing and Toisan. The Tengs' softly spoken, sophisticatedly inflected Mandarin sounded like a sleek, chauffeur-driven town car cruising Sutton Place. The Engs' proudly and loudly shouted street vendor–cadenced Toisan Cantonese was like the screechy, body- and soul-shaking rumblings of the 7 train. Through Gene's marriage, The Eng Dynasty had its first contact with other parts of Manhattan besides Chinatown, and also with different types of Chinese people besides Toisanese.

"So, what are your hobbies?" inquired Gene's future brother-in-law, Peter, at their first meeting.

"I'm a big Met fan," proudly proclaimed Gene, thinking Tom Seaver, Casey Stengel, and Shea Stadium.

"Oh, I try to get to The Met whenever I can," replied Gene's future brother-in-law with approval. "What are your favorite operas?"

In November, sibling #3 (and #2 son), Vic, married Judy Soo Hoo, a Chinese American girl from an exotic land called Flatbush, Brooklyn. At that time, Brooklyn and Queens may as well have been separate universes. (To some, this notion still prevails.) The Soo Hoos were of similar Toisan lineage to The Eng Dynasty, and Judy also shared Vic's edgier outlook. Together, Vic and Judy brought street-smart 1960s counterculture values to the Old World, conservative Eng Dynasty.

As a teenager, Vic was a drummer, and his rock 'n' roll band, The Missing Links, was the first of a long line of bands to rehearse and annoy the neighbors from within the two-car garage of The First Flushing Palace. Vic's biggest Missing Links moment was playing the late Charlie Watts's strutting "tap-tap, tap-tap-tap" rhythms between the fabled "no, no, no's" and "hey, hey, hey's" in The Rolling Stones' "Satisfaction." During the Vietnam War era, Vic frequently came to the dinner table in full hippie regalia—hair down to his shoulders and putting up the peace sign. Seated next to him, Gene sometimes took meals in full ROTC military uniform. I looked at this juxtaposition and thought, "There's something happening here." In time, Gene's and Vic's opposing worldviews would remain as conflicted and divided as the decade in which they were formed. Sadly, their relationship would only worsen from there.

These divergent dispositions also informed their career paths. Gene became a chemical engineer with Domino Sugar—first in Williamsburg, Brooklyn, and then in Baltimore. Vic co-founded Bonsai Dynasty, one of New York's first retail stores for bonsai trees—first in Flushing and then on the corner of 30th Street and 6th Avenue in Manhattan. Herman and I worked many long days and years in Bonsai Dynasty. In many ways, Vic's store was like the second coming of our family's hand laundry.

Being the only daughter of an Old World Chinese family that was only one generation removed from having that unspoken notion of putting daughters either down the river or up for grabs, Jane was fiercely independent. She was the first to permanently move beyond The First Flushing Palace. She went away to college in upstate Oswego, New York, married a non-Chinese, and never again lived in the Flushing/NYC area.

Jane married Mark Lavonas, her Lithuanian American college sweetheart, in Oswego on December 6, 1970, the day before the twenty-ninth anniversary of the attack on Pearl Harbor. For the first few summers of their marriage, Herman and I were invited for extended summer visits—first in Oswego and then in the village of Canastota—one New York State Thruway exit south of Syracuse. Herman and I came to be warmly regarded as that village's "Fresh Air Fund" kids from the big city. Many years later, during the 1990s, Mark would become a multi-term Republican mayor of Canastota. During his '90s reign, the townsfolk referred to their Chinese American first lady as "Hillary," as Jane was a staunch Democrat.

When Jane got married, I was all of eight years old. I could not fathom why Dad and The Empress Mother were *not* going to her wedding. I also could not fathom why they were roaming the laundry like wounded lions roaring, *"Mai ngooy ngoo-wee la."* ["She's not my daughter anymore."] This was not something we talked about, not that we ever talked that much. The silence at most Eng Dynasty meals was deafening.

At Thanksgiving dinner, the week before Jane and Mark's wedding, Gene announced that he and Vic were leading a caravan of family and friends upstate to attend their wedding. As they were both newly married and, as Dad would like to quote the old R&B song, "already 3 × 7," parental permission was no longer an issue. The real issue was whether Herman and I would be allowed to join the caravan.

"Jo-Sahn" ["Good morning"]," I said as I sat down to breakfast in the laundry on the following Friday morning—the day before Gene and Vic's caravan was to take off for upstate New York. I sat down even more meekly than usual and deftly avoided any eye contact with Dad or The Empress Mother. Herman had shrewdly gone to school early that morning.

"Are you going upstate with your brothers to Janie's wedding?" Dad asked, point-blank.

Without looking up, I just nodded my head yes.

We then went on to eat what felt like the longest, most intense breakfast in the thirty-year history of the Foo J. Chin Hand Laundry—if not the 300-year history of Flushing.

My soft spoonfuls of oatmeal never seemed more difficult to swallow. As not a word was spoken and all eye contact was avoided, a perfect storm seemed to be brewing in Dad's mind as every crunching bite of his shredded wheat grew louder and louder. The Empress Mother looked around and frowned. While they never said yes, Dad and The Empress Mother never said no. The next day, a Saturday—the busiest day of the week for the laundry—Herman and I joined Gene and Vic's upstate-bound caravan of family and friends for Jane and Mark's wedding. That was the first time Herman and I had ever defied our parents. It was also the first time that Gene had publicly defeated Dad.

Though only two years prior, my act of defiance to attend Jane and Mark's wedding seemed like a millennium ago as Dad and I sat alone in a void during The Empress Mother's "disappearing act." By now, Herman was well into his teenage fast years and seldom home. Though the long, tense night was ripe for physical violence, Dad never once hit me. Ever. Instead, Dad hit the bottle.

He spent those long Empress Mother–less nights attacking his youngest son with tension-building silences and stern looks, as he poured shot after shot of Johnnie Walker Red and fired up a steady succession of Robert Burns cigarillos. Dad smoked and drank into the night, watching shows like *Gunsmoke* and *Columbo* on TV. Seeing him so absorbed into his scotch, cigarillos, and TV, I felt as if Dad wished he were in *Gunsmoke's* Wild West. I could picture him at the bar knocking back shots with Sheriff Dillon and Festus, with Miss Kitty faithfully setting up round after round. Or maybe Dad wished he were out solving crimes and chomping cigars with TV detective Columbo? But most probably Dad wished he were alone in New York's Chinatown Bachelor Society, back in the days before The Empress Mother caught up with him . . . before he was stuck with all of us.

At three in the afternoon on the third day of one of her disappearances, The Empress Mother reappeared, still wearing her haunting red dress, and had one simple question for Dad.

"*Ngem gafair?*" ["Want some coffee?"]

The Empress Mother asked this at exactly 3:00 P.M., the hour of their daily coffee break, and the time Herman and I came home from school. In a twelve-hour-a-day, six-day workweek, 3 o'clock coffee was something special. Though we hardly said a word to each other, just sitting together, having our coffee, pastries, and a few moments of peace from the work and the world was something to be cherished. Two generations of Eng Dynasty workers who staffed the Foo J. Chin Chinese Hand Laundry always looked forward to 3 o'clock and The Empress Mother's asking, "*Ngem gafair?*"

But on this day, The Empress Mother was asking this cherished question from the other side, the public, customer side of the laundry. Today, *Ngem gafair* didn't mean "Want some coffee?" It meant, "Can I come home?"

Dad, seated at his front workstation, looked up with an air of disgust.

The Empress Mother's eyes avoided his.

Then, just short of saying something stupid, Dad nodded his head, yes.

The Empress Mother lifted up the countertop trap door, unlocked the gate below, and crossed the threshold from the public customer side and back into the private family side. After securing the hatches behind her, she went to the kitchen in the back of our laundry and made the 3 o'clock coffee.

Subsequent disappearing acts followed. *"Ngem gafair"* became The Empress Mother's official declaration that they were over. These declarations were always made at exactly 3 o'clock in the afternoon of the third day of her disappearance. When The Empress Mother decided to end her disappearing acts altogether, she burned the red dress she wore for these "disappearances" in a garbage can in the parking lot behind our laundry. It was a private ceremony. But I watched through the grease-stained, metal-reinforced windowpanes of the back door of the laundry's family area and my own tear stained and fear-filled eyes.

As painful as The Empress Mother's disappearing acts were, we always felt that she would come home. Thankfully, after three days, she always did. But when Dad would retaliate and start to pull off some disappearing acts of his own, all bets were off.

"Ai-ya! Ai-ya!" ["Oh no! Oh no!"] The Empress Mother would wail.

Search parties organized by Vic and Herman would scour The City in search of Dad. While they never told me where they found him, I definitely know where we lost him; we lost Dad in the silence. The silence that followed him home to our laundry, where his disappearing acts, The Empress Mother's disappearing acts, and our grief over both of their disappearing acts were never discussed. Instead, Dad cruised around Flushing in his shiny new Chrysler Newport with the radio turned up loud. His favorite song of this period was Ricky Nelson's "Garden Party." He never missed a chance to sing along with the song's chorus:

"But it's all right now, I learned my lesson well.

See, you can't please everyone, so you've got to please yourself."

Dad worked up until the day he was diagnosed with cancer in November 1976.

On the first Sunday of 1977, Dad entered True Light for the first time since Gene's wedding in 1970. He entered the church to be baptized Lutheran so he and The Empress Mother could both one day be buried together in the Lutheran Cemetery in Glendale, Queens. As The Empress Mother and I once again sat in one of True Light's front pews, Vic and Herman helped Dad, a trembling, cancer-stricken aberration of himself, up to the altar to be baptized. Dad may have brought Gene into this world, but he was leaving it on Gene and The Empress Mother's terms.

Cancer took Dad's life four months later on April 15, 1977: tax day in the U.S.A. I was fourteen when Dad died. This was the same age The Empress Mother was when they had their arranged marriage.

Just before they closed the casket at Dad's funeral, I placed his beloved piece of pierced American currency in his pocket. Now, no government, no laws, no in-laws, village elders, wife, or children could touch it or him. The quarter with a hole right through George Washington's temple, his pierced two-bits, was his for eternity.

Chapter 7

Chinese Rocks

Opium, the Chinese Diaspora and Soul . . . and Punk Rock

SOME HAVE SAID that changing one note or chord has the power to completely alter the compositional balance of a song, symphony, or any piece of music. The same can be said for the structural impact of changing one word in any written, spoken, sung, or lived experience. Now double that and imagine the power that two words can have . . . on a teenager's life. In my teenage high school years, two words, "Chinese Rocks," wreaked havoc on my existence. This havoc also had historical precedence—globally and personally—that I am still processing.

After Dad died, everything changed for The Eng Dynasty. We sold our laundry and The First Flushing Palace—the only home I had ever known. Our investment or rental property that we, or at least I, had come to consider a nuisance and beneath us, was now our new downsized Second Flushing Palace on the *other* side of town. We moved across the Union Street fissure that demarcated the neighborhood's then-predominantly Gentile suburban private-home district to settle into the predominantly Jewish urban district that consisted of apartment buildings and multi-family homes.

The Empress Mother had retired. She was finally the full-time homemaker I'd so wanted her to be when I was a child. Not surprisingly, after Dad's passing and the end of thirty years of a grinding twelve-hours-a-day, six-days-a-week Chinese hand laundry proprietorship—compounded by a combustible 24/7 arranged marriage—The Empress Mother found the peace of mind and improved health that had eluded her for most of her life. Even in our downsized Second Flushing Palace.

When Dad died, I was fourteen. Moving into teenagehood, the child often finds that longing to belong often goes hand-in-hand with one's music and pop culture choices and allegiances. This would prove particularly powerful and polarizing for a little brother growing up in the big shadow of an older brother who was now one of the neighborhood's more talked-about rock 'n' roll guitarists. But this shadow got a little smaller when Herman moved out into his own apartment. For the first time in my life, I had a bedroom of my own. For a teenager, this is a major liberation. I could choose any and all posters that graced the wall, as well as which vinyl LPs and singles that were to be played on the stereo, a.k.a. the twentieth-century record player. But as we know, freedom for a teenager can be a dangerous, if delightful, thing. While The Empress Mother was settling nicely into retirement and Herman into his new apartment and life, I was entering those difficult high school teenage years.

In 1977, I wasn't a child anymore. By the late 1970s, New York was also a completely different city from what it had been even in the early 1970s. While the city was never quite innocent, by the mid-1970s it had become palpably intimidating. New York City was on the verge of going bankrupt financially. We were already bankrupt from a moral and morale point of view. Chaos reigned in the streets and in the souls of New York City. It was in this apocalyptic environment that I entered the brave new world of Flushing High School. But I wasn't alone.

Flushing High School (FHS) is an imposing nineteenth-century Gothic structure, with intimidating gargoyles (the school's mascot) perched atop nearly every tower. It has proudly stood on the corner of Union Street and Northern Boulevard since 1875. Arguably its most famous alum is a work of television fiction—Archie Bunker, the Queens everyman bigot of the 1970s sitcom *All in the Family*.

In the fall of 1977, The Eng Dynasty was still reeling from Dad's passing the previous spring while New York City was rehabbing from a most calamitous summer. That summer saw a citywide blackout that resulted in crimes and looting on a spectacular scale, as well as the capture of a notorious serial killer, Son of Sam, a.k.a. David Berkowitz. Berkowitz's year-long killing spree exclusively terrorized the outer boroughs. The once-proud Flushing High, like all of NYC, was shaken and brought to its knees. During this time, it was not unusual to walk by FHS and see books, chairs, and God knows what else flying out of the windows and crashing down onto the street below. Every year it seemed as if more kids were hanging out outside of the school than actually going in. This would prove to be the perfect petri dish to culture another attempt to circumvent convention: my own punk rock bands. Only this time I had an unlikely accomplice: the Punk Buddha of the 1970s Outer Boroughs, Ray Wong.

There was no missing Ray around Flushing. A heavyset guy with hair halfway down his back, he was always wearing mirrored or equally dazzling shades, a number of bizarre earrings, and a five-pound set of keys on his jeans. He cruised around the neighborhood on bicycle and, later, motorcycle equivalents of pimp-mobiles. Clamped to the bike's frame was an enormous "ghetto blaster" radio adorned with every tacky 1970s car accessory you could think of—including Playboy Bunny air fresheners. The garage where he created and maintained his pimped-out vehicles and received audiences came to be known as Flushing's legendary "Ray's World."

As a Teenage Emperor of Flushing, I thought: Here's a cool Chinese guy who is not on TV, not in the movies, but right here in the flesh and blood in Flushing. He doesn't even know martial arts and everyone still thinks he's cool! He's like Kwai Chang Caine's nonviolently kicking ass for the entire show and not just the final ten minutes. Although we became fast friends in FHS, our first meeting was a year prior and went something like this:

"Hey, your name is Ray, right?" I asked while extending my hand.

Ray left that faux imperial hand hanging, lit up a Marlboro, stared me right in the eye, and slowly raised his middle finger in a most 1970s anti-salute.

Stunned, I rescinded my hand and mumbled, "Man, wh-wh-what was that?"

"Fuck you!" Ray bellowed.

"Whoa, just—"

"Fuck you!" Ray bellowed again.

"—Calm down!"

"Fuck you! Fuck you!! Fuck you!!!" concluded Ray, who got up and promptly peeled out on his pimp-cycle, leaving me high and dry, my unshaken hand now shaking.

Before Ray turned the corner, he treated me to an exclusive viewing of the whole of his moon as he dropped his pants and let his formidable bare cheeks throw caustic caution to the wind as a way of waving goodbye. I soon noticed that Ray's neighborhood cruises often ended with him cursing and/or mooning anyone who got in his way.

We met again the following winter, my final one in The First Flushing Palace, when we were both part of a Bleeker Junior High School entertainment caravan that went to retirement homes around Flushing. I was there to provide acoustic guitar accompaniment for aspiring folk singer classmates, who performed sing-along versions of folk standards, such as "Michael, Row the Boat Ashore," as well as contemporary 1970s hits . . . "Everybody Was Kung Fu Fighting." To my shock, Ray was onboard the caravan as a violinist in a string quartet! On a lunch break, we finally had the conversation that I had tried to initiate the summer before.

"Hey, Ray," I began, this time keeping my hand to myself.

Ray acknowledged me with a nod of his head—abusing no other body parts in this salutation.

"It's nice to play for the old folks, ain't it?" I tentatively started our second conversation.

"It's O.K. . . . . It's better to be out of school for the day," assessed Ray, cutting through what Pink Floyd would call my "do goody good bullshit."

"That's good too," I agreed.

"Can you really play that thing, or are you just faking it to get out of school?" Ray questioned.

"I'm no Pete Townshend, but I can play a little," I humbly defended myself.

"Then, let's play something," challenged Ray.

We put down our soggy sandwiches and picked up our shiny instruments. After some initial noodling, we fell into a lilting, country western–flavored campfire sing-along fiddle and guitar groove. But with each passing of the 12-bar/1-4-5 chord progression, the groove became a competition to see who could be more outrageous—reaching rollicking and satirical punk rock proportions. We laughed until we were literally in tears.

"We should play that at the next stop," I enthused.

"Yeah, show them that not all of us Chinese are nice boys," ripped Ray.

My eyes lit up.

"Who are good in math!" I immediately added.

"Or want to be doctors!"

"Lawyers!"

"Engineers!"

We both knew we had found lifelong blood-brother comrades. Together, we were prepared to take on the dual labyrinth of Flushing High School and the New York City public school system. By the late 1970s, the 1950s Eisenhower Americana Dream and 1960s Civil Rights movement ideologies had both come up empty for our bankrupt generation. We saw no future. To many, these two ideals had even become the butt of ongoing cynical jokes . . . but who was the joke really on?

During my first semester at Flushing High, one fiscal crisis–defining "class" was a physical education outpost that consisted of an overflow bunch of us leaving the gym every morning to walk to a nearby field. This outpost was a result of nearly double the capacity of students being registered for this "class." At the nearby field, the majority of the class smoked cigarettes and all of us drank our morning coffees. And that was *all* we did. One morning, an emergency struck . . . tickets were going on sale for a Cheap Trick concert . . . by the time the school day was over, all tickets would be gone!

"Mr. Shev . . . ," I summoned our Phys. Ed. teacher.

"Shevlin, please . . .," he responded.

"Mr. Shev . . . ," I continued. "It's rare that I would ask a favor of you, but we have an emergency on our hands."

"An emergency?" he replied with a suspicious but playful grin.

"Yes. Tickets have just gone on sale for Cheap Trick at The Palladium in The City. Cheap Trick is one of the greatest rock bands in the world and by the end of the school day, this concert will be sold out . . . think you can maybe lend us thirty dollars to buy four tickets . . . let me run over to the Wacky Weed head shop on Main Street to buy tickets at that Ticketron. . . ."

By this time, our teacher was chuckling aloud.

"I swear I'll pay you back tomorrow . . . and if I leave now, I won't be late for my next class."

Without hesitation, he reached into his pocket, pulled out his wallet, and lent me the money.

"But I'm not writing you a late pass for your next class."

"Thank you, Mr. Shevlin—you're the best!"

I graciously accepted his loan, ran over to Wacky Weed, and scored my Cheap Trick tickets. The next day I paid him back with interest—his favorite coffee and a pack of cigarettes for my now-favorite Phys. Ed. teacher. At least at Flushing High, I was learning how to appeal to people for who they were and not for what they were.

That Phys. Ed. outpost was symbolic of my first months at Flushing High School. During that time, I also took that long walk across the ideological schoolyard from the jocks' side to the heads' side. The jocks were, of course, the athletes. The heads? Let's just say they indulged in less-athletic activities. I no longer wanted to be Willis Reed; I wanted to be Lou Reed. The likes of The Velvet Underground were clearly overtaking the likes of the New York Knicks in my evolving purview.

Lou Reed, Keith Richards of The Rolling Stones, and Johnny Thunders, formerly of The New York Dolls, became my Holy Triumvirate of punky junky rock 'n' roll idols. The public personas and lyrics of these three artists were celebrated just as much for their association with heroin as for their own considerable craft: personifying and objectifying the sexy danger that was 1970s "heroin chic"—from the punk rock vantage. These punky junky idols gave me intellectual freedom. Flesh and blood emancipation from conforming to neighborhood heavy metal and progressive/classic rock rituals came via David Johansen—Thunders's former bandmate and lead singer of The New York Dolls. In the 1980s, Johansen would go on to Top 40 and bar mitzvah/wedding repertoire infamy with "Hot, Hot, Hot" from his ingenious Buster Poindexter persona that was a unique triangulation of equal parts Dean Martin, Jerry Lewis, and 1970s punk insouciance. On the silver screen, Johansen also portrayed the coolest and funniest "Ghost of Christmas Past" alongside Bill Murray in the alternative *It's a Beautiful Life* Christmas classic *Scrooged*.

I first became curious about Johansen after coming face-to-face with him during the winter of my first year of high school at the 30th Street "music building," just south of Madison Square Garden, where hundreds of bands rehearsed. I was there to hear one of Herman's bands rehearse. Coincidentally, I went on a beer run during the same time that Johansen did. Getting carded for beer purchases was a rarity in late-'70s NYC. So together, Johansen and I rode the elevator down and walked to the deli and back without saying a word to each other. Or at least I thought it was him.

After Herman's band rehearsal we got in the elevator to leave and, again, there was David Johansen! This time, one of Herman's bandmates, energized by a great rehearsal and a few good beers, yelled out, "Hey, you look like a Doll!" Johansen smiled his "Butch from *The Little Rascals*" smile (one that The Kinks' Ray Davies has so eloquently described as "looking like it's gonna get what's coming to it") and growled, "Check out my new solo album, it's coming out next month." It really was him! A month later I bought his self-titled solo album. The moment the needle found its groove in the vinyl, I found a new groove for my post-Dad, post-laundry self. "Funky But Chic" and the entire *David Johansen* album was the final step of building my self-confidence to finally step out of my big brother's shadow. It also helped exorcise some of the inner demons of that cowering, browbeaten Pu Yi (China's real Last Emperor) or *Tommy* rock opera man-child that still held me captive from within. The *David Johansen* album had all of punk rock's directness and vitality, yet it also contained a sophisticated and humorous New York wit, swing, and swagger. This unusual combination seemed to crystallize a class-bridging cool for all boroughs and strata of New York City that few artists ever achieve in any genre or medium. Seeing Johansen perform live on stage was the final rite in my joining a new flock of Johansen devotees.

I first saw Johansen perform when he was opening for former Deep Purple guitar god Ritchie Blackmore's Rainbow, at the Asbury Park Convention Center in Bruce Springsteenville, New Jersey. A number of us drove all the way down to the Jersey Shore from Flushing, Queens, only to find out that Blackmore, a legendary diva, had canceled. The David Johansen Group—who proudly introduced themselves as hailing from Staten Island—still agreed to play . . . for free! For their troubles, Johansen & Co. were lustily booed by the departing

Blackmore/Rainbow faithful. This booing throng included many of Herman's bandmates—the pantheon of the older guard in the neighborhood rock 'n' roll hierarchy. This posse collectively condemned The David Johansen Group by asserting:

"Ugh, they suck. They even look like a punk band!"

"What's wrong with that?" I countered.

As most of my Flushing friends stayed in local heavy metal and progressive-rock cliques, I dove headlong into the punk rock and new wave scenes percolating over in "The City." Yes, while the heavy metal/prog rockers—of which Herman was a prominent player—were very talented and had tons of technique . . . they simply weren't funky but chic. And essentially, the heavy metal and progressive-rock bands were saying to their audiences, "Look what *we* can do." At the other end of the rock 'n' roll spectrum, punk/new wave bands were saying, "Look what *you* can do. Anyone can play these three-chord songs . . . so get to it—just have something to say!"

Befitting NYC's bankrupt, crumbling infrastructure, this punk/new wave DIY (do it yourself) ethos was, if not a completely fresh breath of air, a breath of less-polluted air for school-bored, street-savvy teens of the late 1970s. The need to acquire the hard-sought musical and technical craft that Herman's generation had worked very hard to achieve, while greatly respected, was no longer the sole standard by which teens could get their musical groove on and express themselves. Suddenly, limited musical skills but a strong lyrical and stage presence were enough to get on with it. I soon became a regular at all of

Johansen's tri-state-area shows. Within a few months, I even became part of his show . . . sort of.

When The David Johansen Group would break into their rough and ready rendition of The Four Tops' "Reach Out (I'll Be There)," Johansen would go into the audience and get people to sing the "I'll Be There" refrain with him. For many shows, he would do this from atop my shoulders. We had our routine down. During the extended second chorus of "Reach Out (I'll Be There)," I would take off my glasses and hand them to my buddy Sheldon King. Then I would barrel to the front of the stage and turn around in front of Johansen. He would mount my shoulders, and off into the frenzied club we would go—going as far as the mic cable would allow. (This was in the waning days of the pre-wireless, analog age.)

As a result of my acting as his mosh pit camel, Johansen began to receive our Flushing High School entourage backstage. On one of those occasions he also agreed to be interviewed! Afterward, Johansen even dispensed some decidedly un-punk advice.

"Thanks for the interview," I concluded.

"No problem," replied Johansen. "It's for your school paper, right?"

"Yeah."

"That's great," noted Johansen.

"Yes and no," I lamented. "I wish I didn't have to go back to school. I wish I could just drop out and go out on the road with you—"

"Al," Johansen interrupted me with a surprisingly serious tone. "Just get it over with."

∎∎∎

The day that interview was published in Flushing High School's newspaper, *The Flushing Forum*—for which I was features editor—was one of the clearest days of my oft-foggy teenage years. It was December 1979. I was halfway through my senior year of high school with no particular place to go. A new decade beckoned just around the bend. The road beyond Flushing and Flushing High School was calling, screaming even, but I couldn't quite hear it. I knew I had to graduate, but I wasn't feeling it. I knew I had to go to college, but I wasn't feeling it. The thing that made me feel most alive in that moment was seeing my name in print alongside David Johansen's.

Around this time, my brothers Herman and Vic started calling me "T-Boy"—the T standing for Trouble. Herman and Vic were most alarmed by my wildly inconsistent grades, which usually consisted of a 96 in Journalism and failing to barely passing grades in every other subject. These shaky grades triggered letters home to The Second Flushing Palace—warning that my Flushing High graduation could be in peril. As these letters were in English, Herman, boldly stepping up in Dad's absence, would read them for The Empress Mother. In turn, Herman would summon "what are you gonna do with your life" summits in the basement of my brother Vic's store, Bonsai Dynasty. Located on the corner of 30th Street and 6th Avenue in Manhattan, Bonsai Dynasty was, as far as I know, the first retail store to specialize in bonsai trees in The City. Herman was already working there, and soon both Ray and I would join the staff. But for now, Bonsai Dynasty's basement replaced the Foo J. Chin Hand Laundry family back room, where, years earlier, Herman and Dad had lectured me on righting my misguided *Kung Fu* troubles in grade school. Now, Herman and Vic were trying to right my misguided high school rock 'n' roll dreams.

"What do you want to do?" Herman would ask.

"I want to write," I would reply.

"Write what?" Vic would interrogate.

"I want to write . . . rock articles," I finally confessed. "You know, be a rock journalist."

"You really should find something more reliable," advised Herman.

"Alvin, that ain't doing dick, and you know it," summarized Vic. "Look, if you're not going to pay attention at school, you may as well come here every day. Help me and help yourself make some money."

■■■

In Flushing High and throughout the NYC public school system of the late 1970s, most of us knew that we were on our own to educate and emancipate ourselves. But while the gaining of conventional academic knowledge and education at FHS was, at least for me, scarce, there was an abundance of real world or street-smart lessons to be learned . . . such as the influence of being a member of the press.

Among my dubious electives during my troubled senior year was Auto Mechanics Shop. How or why I chose this elective, I don't quite remember. But I will never forget how I got out of it.

"You're gonna have to do better," warned the auto shop teacher, as he returned yet another failed test to me. Ironically, he also doubled as the Phys. Ed. teacher, who actually kept the students in the gym and tested them on their physical prowess—rather than shepherding the overflow group to smoke cigarettes and drink coffee in an adjacent field. After gazing at yet another failing test grade, I noticed a poster on the bulletin board promoting an upcoming Automotive Vocational seminar for high school students. I had an idea.

"Uh, excuse me," I caught my teacher's attention—pumping the gas on the courage engine to see if there wasn't another way to a passing grade.

"What is it?" honked the auto shop teacher.

"I write for the school paper, *The Flushing Forum* . . . and I was thinking that maybe I can write an article about that upcoming Automotive Vocational seminar in the paper. Maybe that will help get some more students interested."

"That would be great," the auto shop teacher high-beamed.

"And do you, uh, think that could help my grade?"

"Well . . ." pondered the auto shop teacher, shifting to neutral. "I think it will."

A month later, the auto shop teacher got his article. Two months later, I got my passing grade of 65 in Auto Mechanics Shop . . . and my graduation was assured. Although my brothers and I obviously disagreed about the merits and prospects of a career in rock journalism, I was starting to see some of its tangible benefits.

Shortly before Christmas, I packed many extra copies of my prized *Flushing Forum* profile of David Johansen, boarded the #7 train, and headed into Manhattan for what would be Johansen's last show of the 1970s. I was heading to the city with hopes of having my hero autograph my article. The show was held at

Irving Plaza, the Ukrainian dance hall that had been converted into a punk rock emporium just east of Union Square in Lower Manhattan's tony Gramercy Park. Johansen and the band were in their usual fine form. Then came the evening's real challenge: getting backstage.

After the final encore, The New York Dolls' rousing arrangement of Bo Diddley's "Pills," I joined the backstage queue. Already a recognizable face to Johansen's crew and entourage, I used the first acknowledgment of eye contact to stake my claim:

"Look, I wrote this," I pleaded, while thrusting the article into the face of the roadie guarding the backstage door.

"David said to show it to him when it came out," I further pleaded my case.

The rock 'n' roll sentry considered this claim and magically moved me and a few friends out of the sweaty hordes and into the promised land beyond the vaunted velvet ropes.

After we found and felt our way down a dark and narrow passageway filled with empty musical equipment cases, there was Johansen, exhausted from a high-energy performance and feeling no pain from God knows what else. He gave our crew an absolutely giddy welcome. Then, even in this delirious state, he *read* the article . . . and found a most embarrassing typo.

"You called me 'impotant,'" accused Johansen. "I think you mean 'impoRtant,' right?"

Big awkward silence . . .

"I don't know how we missed that," I conceded, my face turning beet red.

Johansen and his entourage broke into hysterical laughter.

"Don't worry, Al. It's Christmas," consoled Johansen, who autographed the article anyway, adding a finishing flourish of a big blue "R."

▟▟▟

Concurrent with my David Johansen mania, I started seriously practicing on one of the guitars that Herman had left behind and, of course, started my own Johansen/New York Dolls–inspired band. As rock 'n' roll was in my soul but never quite in my fingers—in complete contrast to Herman—late-1970s punk rock's DIY axis fit me and Ray like a second-hand hipster suit—a garment we were both in constant pursuit of. As I would go on to emulate the guttural guitar stylings of my holy triumvirate heroes—Lou Reed, Keith Richards, and Johnny Thunders—Ray took up the bass and started calling himself "Leslie Wong" after Leslie West, the stout namesake guitarist/singer of the great NYC band Mountain. By the way, "West" was actually born Leslie Weinstein in Forest Hills, Queens. With outer boroughs pride and distorted bass guitar shout-outs, "Leslie Wong" never missed an opportunity to play Leslie West's signature "Mississippi Queen" guitar solo on his bass while plugged into two fuzz boxes and a *wah-wah* pedal.

Together we started to front inspired but, shall we say, musically challenged garage bands. By now, I had grown to almost 6' tall, had shed most of my baby fat, and was sporting long hair that spiked on top. When I was playing next to the shorter, rounder, dark-bespectacled, and outrageously punk/biker–attired Ray "Leslie" Wong, we hardly resembled the classic Jagger–Richards or Johansen–Thunders rock duo image. But we did begin to attract our fair share of attention.

Soon Ray and I were the rhythm and bass guitarists in Howard Turk and The Grips. Yes, The Grips shamelessly modeled or, depending on your perspective, stole our entire stage attitude and gig structure from Johansen and his band. Only, our band

was awful. Yet through these bands, and our mutual love of
rock 'n' roll and the rock 'n' roll lifestyle, I finally had a peer
group and fit in somewhere.

Like Lou, Keith, and Johnny, my clothes were black. Like
Queen's Freddie Mercury, my fingernails were painted black
. . . and Ray and I were the only ones in the band, and in our
punky circle, who didn't have to dye our hair black. Everyone
had these big rooster haircuts and we were cool. Everything
was cool until I heard about the song "Chinese Rocks."

As implausible as it seems, those two little words, "Chinese
Rocks," instantly reduced me back into that Last Emperor Pu
Yi/*Tommy* trance-like vortex. It was as if my entire being was
transported back to the back room of the Foo J. Chin Hand
Laundry. I could even hear The Empress Mother declaring,

"Mo ho ngen oh nguy-tie.
Um tek ngen.
Alloy no ho-gnen oh-key.
Mo ho ngen oh nguy-tie."

[There's no good people out there.
They don't feel for people.
All the good people you will ever need are right here at
    home.
There are no good people out there.]

Here, I thought, I had finally reinvented myself as a punky
junky wannabe that actually fit in somewhere. I thought I'd
never have to see, and certainly never have to *be*, that stunted
Tommy or Last Emperor/Pu Yi guy again. By that point, I fig-
ured I'd left him behind, way behind, back on the jocks' side of
the "pre–Funky But Chic/heroin chic" schoolyard. In an instant,
it no longer mattered that The Grips had reached the pinnacle
of that fishbowl of a universe that was Flushing High School. It
didn't matter that one of the smartest and prettiest girls in the

school was on my arm. All that mattered was that by just reading this song title on an album cover I felt betrayed by the very movement that I thought had liberated me from my primal identity crises. Was "Chinese Rocks" mocking my ethnicity? Was I really not welcome to the punk rock party after all?

When I finally got the courage to actually listen to "Chinese Rocks," I heard that the song, co-written by the aforementioned former New York Doll Johnny Thunders and The Ramones' Dee Dee Ramone, was about scoring heroin. China White heroin. By this time, I had also started smoking pot and drinking beer. But for whatever reason, I never quite took it to the next level—though I certainly harbored heroin chic fantasies inspired by my Holy Triumvirate of Punky Junky Idols. In short, I spent my late-1970s teenage years as a real "heroin chic junky-wannabe." I guess you could say I wanted to "do the time but was very afraid of doing the crime." Somehow, I acquainted this inability to take something all the way—even when it may not have been such a good thing to take all the way—as yet another form of the Queens quandary mindset of living in the perennial state of being so close, yet so far away from, the *real thing*. The *real thing* being any association with "The City"— which is what we late-'70s/late-twentieth-century outer boroughs kids will always call Manhattan. Back then, Manhattan was the undisputed center of the arts and cultural universe. This was a half-century before real estate evened the cultural score and made Brooklyn the reigning Kingsborough of Cool. In that time and in that sense, Queens may as well have been Kansas. Being in a rock 'n' roll band helped bridge this Queens quandary—if only in my mind.

Of course, my black-nail-polished rock 'n' roll junky wannabe fantasy would get shattered every night when I'd return to The Second Flushing Palace to have dinner with The Empress Mother. She would just look at my black fingernails and in her broken English mutter, "Ha, ha, Batman."

The Empress Mother saw right through my new mask, but she also knew what I was going through. It was going to take a lot of work to create a new life and identity for ourselves, as well as a new relationship as "full-time" mother and son in the post-Dad, post-laundry era.

But that was home, where fantasies usually die. And die ugly, may I add. How did the reality get mixed up with the fantasy?

Was "Chinese Rocks" the poetic price to pay for posing as a "heroin chic junky" wannabe?

Was "Chinese Rocks" the karmic price to pay for the wayward ways of my grandfather who died an opium addict on the streets of New York's Chinatown?

Just as I was the only child whom Dad never physically beat and who was only lightly disciplined by him and The Empress Mother, I was also their only child who was never subject to Dad's intense anti-drug tirades. My four older siblings told me that these takedowns often went into excruciatingly graphic details about our grandfather's opium overdose on the streets of NYC's Chinatown. On that night, Dad had to identify *his* father's body in a morgue. Family legend has it that my grandfather's body was supposedly hanging upside down by a toe hook—like a slab of beef in a meat freezer of a morgue. Naturally, this traumatic event haunted my Dad for the rest of his life. But even though my grandfather died of an opium overdose on the streets of Chinatown, make no mistake about it, he was a casualty of China's Opium Wars with Great Britain. You can never underestimate the impact of opium on China, on the Chinese diaspora, and, perhaps most profoundly, on the Chinese soul and psyche.

Following the Industrial Revolution of the late eighteenth century, and in response to attempts by the British to expand their trade to ports in northern China, the Qing emperor in 1757 issued a decree explicitly ordering that Guangzhou be made the only port opened to foreign commerce. Eventually, to counter the edict, the British found a product that China wanted and did not have: opium.

Starting in 1820, thousands of pounds of opium were being smuggled into China via the Port of Canton. By the 1830s, there were an estimated 12 million opium addicts in China, mostly men under forty and virtually the entire army. In an effort to stop this epidemic, the Ching Dynasty sent representatives south from the Imperial Palace to Canton. There, in an act that echoes the Boston Tea Party, Ching Dynasty officials seized and burned a shipment of British opium—casting its ashes into the Pearl River delta of the South China Sea, very close to my family's ancestral village of Toisan. The officials then declared the Port of Canton, and in turn China, completely closed to foreigners.

In retaliation, the British started what would turn out to be The First Opium War of 1839–42. The First Opium War defeat was the biggest humiliation in Chinese history. The defeat permanently opened China to the West against her will. This opening, in turn, destroyed China's economy and overall image of itself, however insular, of being the "Heavenly Middle Kingdom" that was superior to all others and led by an emperor who was the "Son of Heaven." This defeat was the beginning of the end of the Ching Dynasty and feudal rule in China. Thus, The Opium Wars also indirectly begat China her fabled "Last Emperor," Aisin Gioro Pu Yi.

The victorious British set up five trading ports throughout China. Perhaps the most infamous bounty settlement of The Opium Wars was when Hong Kong became a British colony in 1842. Hong Kong became Britain's base for further military, political, and economic penetrations of China. Hong Kong would remain British until 1997, when it was returned to the People's Republic of China.

This British invasion opened the floodgates for almost a century of colonizing European nations and, later, Japan. With these occupations, poverty, chaos and anarchy swept through the cities, towns, and villages of China. The defeated Ching Dynasty was also too weak to stop a steady, and unprecedented, illegal exodus of people—like my grandfather— through these same ports to the former British colony of the United States of America and other points west. While my grandfather could emancipate himself from the systemic oppression that was the fate of all poor peasants in China, he could not overcome the power of the powder that was the oppression of opium in his native village of Toisan outside of Guangzhou, China, or in his adopted village of Chinatown in New York City.

▚▚▚

By co-writing "Chinese Rocks," Johnny Thunders and Dee Dee Ramone unwittingly tapped into this centuries-old and generations deep primal opium fault line of the Chinese diaspora and The Eng Dynasty. Many years after first hearing and being paralyzed by that song's title, Ray and I attended the funeral of Johnny Thunders—who died way too young at the age of thirty-eight.

Just as Johansen's punk swing hinted at a larger wit and world beyond our teenage punk orbit, Thunders also gave us glimpses of a bigger and different world. Years before acoustic or *unplugged* shows became standard fare for most rockers, Thunders would occasionally put aside the deafening decibels for an acoustic evening at the legendary Mudd Club. There, he'd share the bill with beat poets like Allen Ginsberg and Gregory Corso. This punk–beat generation alliance reflected a common family dynamic ritual of youngest embracing oldest, and vice versa—forming a bond that would ignore the in-between child. In our case, that pesky middle child/in-between generation to be passed over was the Woodstock hippie generation.

But if Johansen's "Funky But Chic" savoir faire made us feel glad to be alive, Johnny Thunders's self-proclaimed "junky business" made us question *why* we were alive. Thunders would begin many a show by announcing, in his inimitable Queens-inflected junky drawl, "O.K., you guys got it: I'm gonna die tonight." And his audience would go berserk! I would never attempt to carry *this* guy on my shoulders.

Thunders's funeral was held on a raw, wet, and cold April Sunday on Northern Boulevard in Bayside, Queens. Yes, Johnny was also from Queens, as was his "Chinese Rocks" co-writer, Dee Dee Ramone. In fact, Johnny was from Bayside—one town east and even farther away from The City than Flushing. He didn't seem to be caught up in any Queens quandary of being born so close, yet so far away from the center of the universe, Manhattan. He didn't settle for standing in the shadows of The City just because he'd been born and raised in Queens. He just up and reinvented himself as the outer boroughs' or "poor man's" version of Keith Richards. And in certain circles, Johnny was the real deal—the ultimate unpredictable anti-hero who was consistently snatching defeat from the jaws of victory. He scored solo, post-Dolls "underground/alternative" hits with "You Can't Put Your Arm Around a Memory," his scorched pavement cover of the Ventures' surf rock classic "Pipeline," and, of course, "Chinese Rocks."

Thunders died as he lived, a mystery. He died at St. Peter's Guest House in New Orleans under criminal circumstances that were never resolved. While drugs were detected in his blood, there were also numerous reports of loud sounds of physical confrontations coming from Thunders's hotel room. Whether these sounds were a result of junky convulsions or a new kid in town being rolled by local drug thugs will never be known. The investigation has been closed.

As Ray and I drove up Northern Boulevard from Flushing to Bayside to attend Thunders's funeral, we passed Flushing High School, the Saravan Diner, and all of the other "Glory Days" spots of our teenage years. I got to thinking of how people come from all over the world to reinvent themselves and become part of the New York City arts world. But what about those of us who just have to take the #7 train? In some ways it's harder to reinvent yourself when your past, and everyone in it, is just a few subway stops away.

Johnny Thunders's funeral was the definition of the Queens quandary. On the left aisle you had all of the outer boroughs "bridge and tunnel" punks (Ray and I included) who were there to mourn Johnny Thunders, and were having a party in doing so. But on the other side of the aisle were the mourners of John Anthony Genzale, the little kid that Johnny Thunders left behind in Queens when he reinvented himself in The City. The Genzale mourners all had dark shadows around their dark, immigrant Italian eyes. Eyes that were bloodshot from crying, "Johnny . . . We hardly knew ya."

This Old World immigrant/Queens semi-hipster divide was very familiar. Too familiar. The sight of the younger mourners squirming uncomfortably betwixt and between Old and New World modes of mourning brought back memories of my own Dad's funeral.

With Dad's passing, we all took on more responsibility to look out for one another—particularly the newly widowed Empress Mother. The first step, all five children of The Eng Dynasty agreed, was that we had to liberate her from standing on Old World rituals of extreme mourning that were not helping any of us through these difficult days—least of all The Empress Mother herself. One such ritual that was starting to physically sicken The Empress Mother was the forced old-school Chinatown funeral ceremony of playing the role of the wailing widow to the hilt whenever Old World relatives and friends arrived. After the first day of receiving mourners, The Empress Mother had literally made herself sick with this "performative grief"— compounding her actual grief. We kids convinced her that she didn't have to, essentially, put on a show. The Empress Mother spent the next two days of receiving mourners in a quieter, more dignified manner that kept her and our spirits up for this most challenging time. After all, in most respects, funerals are for the living.

After taking in and processing the bifurcated Thunders/Genzale funeral scene for a little while longer, I took my turn to pay my last respects to the deceased. As I got within eyesight of the casket, I almost laughed because Johnny Thunders had more color in his face there than I'd ever seen him have when he was alive. Staring at Johnny Genzale/Thunders in his casket also made me think more of that vacant gaze I saw way too often in my own Dad's eyes. I imagined I would have seen this same opium glaze in my grandfather's eyes—before being closed forever by opium. Using the only Chinese gesture of respect and mourning that my parents ever taught me, or at least the only one I remembered, I bowed three times as I stood before Johnny Thunders's casket . . . the first for my dead teenage "heroin chic" punky junky idol, the second for the grandfather I never knew— who crossed oceans, countries, and cultures only to die of an opium overdose on the streets of New York City's Chinatown—and the third for the spirits of both to find the peace and paths to no longer haunt but to continue to inspire me and all of us who follow after them. I never imagined that this is where we would all wind up from "Chinese Rocks."

Chapter 8

∷

A Sort of Homecoming

But Where Are You *Really* From?

"Hong sigh Bah-king!" ["Good enough to walk to Beijing!"]
declared The Empress Mother as she slapped a pair of black
sneakers the way one used to kick the tires of a new automobile.
This was a common expression from her childhood to basically
say, "These boots are made for walkin'." She was choosing what
footwear to pack for our trip to China in 1987. The Empress
Mother was elated that she was going to be the first member
of her family to set foot in Beijing, walk on The Great Wall, and
travel to more parts of China than anyone else in her family or
village. Of course, every journey begins with a significant first
step that can often be quite challenging. As we waited for our
connecting flight to Hong Kong at Narita Airport in Tokyo, The
Empress Mother sat and stewed—arms folded, face
scowling.

"What's wrong?" I asked.

"Ai-yah! Koy yai" ["Oh no! This place is so awful,"] she acidly
observed, while practically spitting on the ground.

All her life, The Empress Mother complained that her arthritis was a result of her having to sleep in cold, wet fields during the Japanese occupation of China. Of those days, The Empress Mother would regularly recount stories that basically translated into:

"If the Communists come, tell them you're a Communist. If the Nationalists come, tell them you're a Nationalist. But if the Japanese come . . . run for your life!!!"

Seeing these still-raw emotions overcome every fiber of The Empress Mother's sixty-seven-year-old body was painful. The Narita stopover couldn't have ended too soon.

Our China tour included tour guides who would meet us at each train station or airport. The guides then escorted us to the hotel and showed us around for a day or two. After we wandered on our own for a day, the guides got us back to the airport or train station. Remember, this was back in the days before China became one of the preeminent international tourist destinations. As such, most of the trains, planes, and stations on our 1987 trip were still of the austere 1950s Soviet military model—as were most of the accommodations and tour guides.

We entered the People's Republic of China via Guangzhou, the capital city of our family's ancestral province of Guangdong, on a train from Hong Kong, which was then still part of the United Kingdom. The station was right in the throbbing heart of the city, which was teeming with markets full of families, farmers, merchants, and hustlers who all seemed to be in loud, heated negotiations 24/7. Back then, city boulevards were the stage for the grand proletariat "bicycle ballet" of endless hypnotic streams of cyclists—most still wearing their gray or blue "Mao uniforms"— transporting everything from furniture to livestock on the back of their bicycles. The cyclists advanced and stopped in sequences that were choreographed by the unforgiving urban Chinese traffic system.

Our arrival in China also coincided with my twenty-fifth birthday—making me a year older than The Empress Mother was when she emigrated to America, essentially solo, as the "paper wife" of a village friend to find her arranged husband. As soon as we got off the train in Guangzhou, The Empress Mother had a wild smile on her face and an uncharacteristic spring in her step as she shouted, *"Fon a kee luh!"* ["We've come home!"]

As The Empress Mother and I walked through the Guangzhou station, she was swaying her head and swinging her handbag like a schoolgirl. It was clear that she'd reconnected with the free spirit she had left behind forty-one years ago. Before she became an arranged wife. Before she became an illegal alien immigrant to America, a mother, a U.S. citizen, a grandmother, and now a widow. Guangzhou is to Toisan what Manhattan is to Flushing. But The Empress Mother refused to go back to our ancestral village in nearby Toisan. She felt that too much time had passed, but perhaps too little water had accumulated under the bridge to float over her turbulent and painful past.

Miraculously, we found our driver in the midst of the cacophony that was the downtown Guangzhou railway station. From there, we were whisked, along with a half-dozen other tourists, all of whom were North American Caucasians, into a waiting mini-bus. With many a sudden stop and outburst of caustic Cantonese cursing, the driver navigated the unyielding throngs of pedestrians and bicyclists along streets dotted with alternating clusters of Chinese city/village street huts and buildings that bore the stamp of colonizing Portuguese architecture.

Finally, the mini-bus pulled onto a wider boulevard, picked up speed, and started cruising alongside the magnificently muddy Pearl River. Before long, we crossed a moat-like threshold and entered one of Guangzhou's pillars of Western-styled tourist opulence: a towering, gleaming white building known as the White Swan Hotel, on the banks of the Pearl River.

But the White Swan wasn't always "The White Swan." Before it was a lavish four-star hotel, it was a rendezvous point for imminently emigrating paper wives and husbands, as well as paper daughters and sons. They would all converge on the White Swan to purchase and pick up their illicit identities of forged I.D. papers and foreign currency. For most of these brave travelers, who were primarily peasant farmers from the Toisan region, this was probably their very last stop in China ever—before rough sailing into the unknown that was the United States of America on the other side of the world. The Empress Mother made this unglamorous journey to the United States forty-one years before to find her arranged husband, whom she had not seen or heard from in more than a decade. As we pulled up to the White Swan, she just broke down and cried at the memory that the building evoked.

That evening's dinner in the White Swan's elegant dining room turned into a celebration of The Empress Mother's homecoming and my turning twenty-five. The festivities concluded with a birthday cake that I couldn't read and a rendition of "Happy Birthday" that I couldn't understand verbally—though its sentiment still makes me smile. After this evening, things would become stranger and even more unfamiliar.

Throughout the trip, The Empress Mother communicated with her countrywomen and men, whether they spoke Mandarin or Cantonese, through writing but not by speaking. This process still befuddles my mind. Everywhere she went, The Empress Mother was treated like returning royalty. My experience and reception led to a very different sort of "homecoming."

From the moment I arrived, I was acutely aware that I was in my mother's land, and not my motherland. In the new world of America, Old World Chinese call us ABCs—American-born Chinese—"*Juk-Sing.*" "*Juk-Sing*" literally means "hollow bamboo" but bluntly implies "dead wood." In the Old World of China, we were treated slightly differently. While we were clearly not one of "us," a "legitimate" son of China, we were also not quite one of "them," a complete *bok-gwai* or *hok-gwai* "white devil" or "black devil" foreigner either.

During a quiet break away from the half-dozen other North Americans in our tour group, I had a curious exchange with the Guangzhou tour guide. Once he was sure the other tourists in our group were gone, his eager-to-please smile and demeanor morphed into the prowling, probing body language of a private investigator on the verge of cracking the case.

He practically got in my face and suspiciously whispered: "I study America. Can I ask you some questions?"

"Sure," I said.

After taking one more look around to make sure that we were still alone, he pleaded:

"Tell me, does this 'Triple K' organization really exist?"

The off-duty tour guide stared me right in the eye, demanding the truth.

I was shocked, my first instinct being to tell a joke to try to lighten the mood à la, "Buddy, if you get a flat tire or have other car trouble in the States, you don't want to call them. . . ."

But quickly realizing that we were in that cultural reference twilight zone of different galaxies eclipsing each other—where no one will get your jokes—I just said, "Yes, they exist and they do all of the things that you've heard about."

As he absorbed this troubling confirmation, I could not imagine him asking other members of the tour group this same question.

Then, as the tour members regrouped around us, his American queries abruptly turned banal, and he was back on duty. It was amazing to see how quickly he transitioned from this troubled man on a mission who was deeply wary of Westerners—Americans in particular—back into the happy-go-lucky tour guide who couldn't be more eager to shepherd Westerners around his hometown of Guangzhou. China instantly became a world I could touch but not feel.

Growing up in my time and in my mind, it was simply an indisputable belief and virtual fact of life that New York City, and by extension the U.S.A., was the center of the universe—the home of the bravest, the brightest, and, of course, the coolest. Well, things are seldom what they seem. But jarring glimpses behind the façade, like this one with the Guangzhou tour guide, made me reexamine things even more closely, especially when one was already in an introspective, transitional, stateless state—personally and professionally.

The year of our China trip, 1987, marked ten years since Dad passed away. This landmark anniversary also coincided with my first professional crossroads of sorts. Although I couldn't fully process it then, by age twenty-five I had already found and outgrown my first dream job in my then dream field of the music industry.

While still attending Queens College, I was able to parlay my Flushing High School journalistic coup of interviewing David Johansen into assignments for several local music papers and fanzines (sort of like analog blogs). These publications, along with a recommendation from Laurie Leherman, a friend from "The Benches," a local schoolyard drinking/pot-smoking hangout, helped me land an internship with A&M Records' publicity department and, ultimately, my first job as a publicity assistant for Island Records. This British/Jamaican record company introduced Bob Marley, Steve Winwood, and U2, among many others, to the world. For a twenty-two-year-old who lived, breathed, and dreamed rock 'n' roll and paid only passing attention to everything else, getting this position was the absolute greatest joy and achievement at that time.

My days were spent pitching stories on Island recording artists to print media outlets, escorting/babysitting rock stars as they made their P.R. rounds, and doling out the "promo" albums and making up the all-important club and party guest lists. It was like being given the keys to the rock 'n' roll fan's goldmine. To also get paid for this, even at an extremely modest entry-level salary, added up to the ultimate fix for a twenty-two-year-old rock 'n' roll junky. Even the usually interminably long 7 train ride from Flushing, Main Street, to Manhattan seemed to zip along as I devoured rock rag after rock rag and related music biz propaganda . . . all for my job! I had found my professional home. Or so I thought.

During those first dazzling months on the job, I started going to all of the exclusive backstage areas of the NYC clubs and concert halls I'd only read about in the rock press. I also started meeting many of the writers behind the bylines I'd been reading for years. During my first month on the job, I even got to shake hands with the aforementioned Mr. Winwood—and it was literally both of them in a jovial four-hands-in-one shake that I took to be some sort of secret Island Records bonding ritual. Winwood looked ever the elegant British gentleman tourist, replete with Macy's shopping bags that were bursting to capacity. The whole time our four hands were one, a mere matter of seconds in real time, all I could think of was: *Wow, these hands played that great organ riff on "Gimme Some Lovin'."*

Through this first professional position, my name and outlook may as well have been "AlvinfromIsland." This is how I identified myself hundreds of times a day on the phone—this was back in the pre-Internet/e-mail days when fax machines were state-of-the-art office technology—as well as at music biz functions and gigs. Island Records was one of the first companies to move into the sleekly renovated loft/office building on 4th

The Eng family in front of the Unisphere at the 1964 World's Fair in Flushing Meadows Corona Park. (*Left to right*) Gene, Herman, Victor, Dad (King Wah Eng), the author, Jane, and Toy Lain Chin Eng (a.k.a. The Empress Mother).

The family with paternal Grandmother Eng, on the front steps of the family's First Flushing Palace. (*Top row*) Victor, Jane, and Gene; (*Middle Row*) Herman, The Empress Mother holding the author, Dad, and his Mother. (1967)

Beside The Empress Mother in our Foo J. Chin Hand Laundry on Union Street in Flushing, Queens, NYC. Photo: Gene Q. Eng. (1968)

Sitting among the dirty laundry piled up around Dad's feet in our laundry, Flushing, Queens, NYC. Photo: Gene Q. Eng. (1968)

The Empress Mother, Jane, and Dad, in front of our laundry. Photo: Gene Q. Eng. (early 1960s)

The Empress Mother as NYC tour guide at the United Nations. The Toisan Village Elders who raised her and her brother (Hong On Wong, not pictured), on their visit from Oakland, California. (*Left to right*) Chun Oy Woo, Art Ming Woo, and The Empress Mother. (1974)

erforming with my teenage band, The Grips, at The Bitter End, Greenwich Village, NYC. (1981)

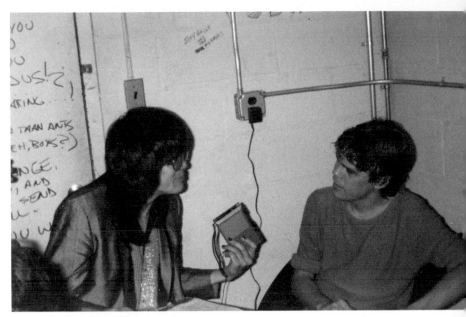

Music biz days: interviewing David Johansen. (1981)

Music biz days: with Lou Reed at a benefit reading for The Writers Voice creative writing program of the Upper West Side YMCA. Four years later, I would take my first playwriting class in that program. Photo: Eb Roberts/© Ebet Roberts. (1984)

Music biz days: working the press room at the New York Music Awards, with (*left to right*) Run, Jam Master Jay, and DMC. Beacon Theatre, NYC. (1987)

With The Empress Mother in Guilin, China, during our "Sort of Homecoming" trip. (1987)

A classroom in Guilin, China, where the students asked the author, "If there was a war between China and the U.S., who would you fight for?" (1987)

From the author's first play: "Big Character Poster," a fictional rock band from China in a fake promo shot for their American debut. (*Left to right*) Ed Chuang, Ray Wong, Valorie Lee, Steve Ning, and the author. Photo: Bethany Eden Jacobson. (1988)

The author with his best teenage friend, Ray Wong, in a short film adaptation of his play *The 20th Anniversary Reunion Concert of Big Character Poster*. Art Direction: Bing Lee. Photo. Nancie Hemminger. (1989)

Poster for *The Goong Hay Kid* at The Nuyorican Poets Café. This was the first play written by an Asian American to be presented at this venerable venue. (*Left to right*) Victoria Linchong, the author, Ken Leung, Alexander Storm. Poster design: Sokie Lee. (1994)

As his punk-rap character, *The Goong Hay Kid*. (1995)

La MaMa, e.t.c. Presents

THE LAST HAND LAUNDRY
IN
CHINATOWN

(A Requiem For American Independents)

A New Musical Drama

Concept, Book & Lyrics by   Music by
ALVIN ENG   ### JOHN DUNBAR

Directed by
BEVYA ROSTEN

Featuring:

EMY BAYSIC, LORI TAN CHINN, RICHARD EBIHARA, JOJO GONZALEZ,
GABRIEL HERNANDEZ, MING LEE, ELIZABETH SPECK

Musical Director   Lighting Designer
MIRIAM DALY   **HOWARD THIES**

Set Designer   Stage Manager   Costume Designer
JOEY MENDOZA   **ALEXANDRA LOPEZ**   **LINDA KELLER**

"You used to have to buy-in, to be an American.
Now you to have to sell-out, to really get some clout."

Workshop Production:
May 9,10,11 & 16,17,18, 1996 - 10 PM

The Club At La MaMa,
74-A East 4th St., NYC
(Betw. 2nd Ave & Bowery)

For further information: (212) 475-7710

Dad's village in Toisan, China. My fiancée, Wendy Wasdahl, and I were on a pilgrimage for a blessing of our marriage. (2007)

Wedding Day, 01.01.08. Wendy in traditional Chinese red for her wedding dress, NYC. Photo: Bard Martin. (2008)

Mother's Day. (*Left to right*) Wendy's mom, Ann Brown, and The Empress Mother in Bowne Park, Flushing, Queens, NYC. (2000)

With my brother Herman in Los Angeles, where he is a musician and guitar technician. (2010)

With Wendy in front of the banner for the "Our Town: HK/USA" Fulbright residency at City University of Hong Kong. (2011)

Wendy and I with City University of Hong Kong students after their performance of "Hong Kong Time Capsule 2011" in the "Our Town: HK/USA" Fulbright residency. (2011)

he author performing "The Last Emperor of Flushing" in his family's ancestral Guangdong province. (2011)

As "The Last Emperor of Flushing" in front of the Unisphere on the former World's Fair Grounds in Flushing Meadows Corona Park, Queens, NYC. Photo: Bellamy. (2006)

Street and Broadway—over the newly opened Tower Records mega-store. Looking back, I see that this building was a harbinger of the extreme gentrification that would come to define the East Village, New York City, and the urban world of the 1980s indeed and in deed.

After some months of heady beginner's luck, I soon found out that advancement in the music biz, and truly making my mark in Manhattan, or "The City" as we children of the outer boroughs will always call it, would not be so easy.

At music industry functions, I was not just the only Chinese kid in the classroom or schoolyard anymore. Now I was also the only one to be living in the then-perceived-to-be-un-hip, culturally impoverished provinces beyond Manhattan. I was once again face-to-face with the Queens quandary of being so close, yet so far away from the center of the universe, The City. Only this time the longing to belong also had professional implications. As an insecure twenty-two-year-old trying to get a foothold in the music biz and The City, I wish I could say I passed all of these tests with flying colors. At many of these functions, after probably overzealously introducing myself as "AlvinfromIsland," I soon recognized a pattern.

Question #2 was usually, "Where are you from?"

"Flushing," I enthusiastically replied.

As many of these music bizzers were themselves New York newcomers, most replied, "Flushing . . . where's that?"

"Out in Queens—last stop on the 7 train," I confirmed.

Then I'd silently count to myself, "1 . . . 2 . . . 3 . . ." and like clockwork, someone inevitably inquired:

"But where are you *really* from?"

"Brian?" was also how I was often greeted at music industry events as many colleagues assumed I was Brian Chin, an R&B/dance music columnist for the music industry "bible," *Billboard*. To my knowledge, he and I were the only Asian Americans in the NYC pop/rock music media at that time. And this wasn't just a NYC music industry thing or even a domestic thing. While I was doing publicity for the historic *One World* music tour that paired Nigerian innovators King Sunny Adé and His African Beats, with the phenomenal Jamaican reggae band Black Uhuru, everyone connected with the latter band called me "Chin" for the entire tour.

For many people, their mid-twenties is when they truly become independent thinkers and beings. This is when one's mind gets a chance to unwind or even mend outside of the two primary institutional structures that had largely defined their identity to date: school and family. After a few years of working as a music publicist, and as my mid-twenties approached, I took a long look at myself and my situation and faced a major professional crossroads:

Did I want to double down in my music P.R. work and strive to become a vice president of publicity for a major record company? . . . Did I want to start my own P.R. firm?

The answer in my heart was a resounding "no" to both questions, as well as to variations on these aspirations. I concluded that while I would be a lifelong rock 'n' roll aficionado, I was only passing through the music business. It was on one of those "still here, but just passing-thru" gigs that, unexpectedly and inexplicably, I turned the corner on dealing with "Where are you *really* from?" and my mid-twenties embodiment of the longing to belong.

In early 1986 I was assigned to be the P.R. account executive for a band that was many miles away from my musical main roads, the Swiss pop-rock/ersatz heavy metal headbangers Krokus. On St. Patrick's Day, I arranged a full meet-the-press day of interviews and other NYC promo events for their lead singer, Marc Storace. This press day morning started off as usual—taking the 7 train into Manhattan. Only on these days, I would bypass the office to wait at the hotel for the rock star of the day's grand, often tardy entrance. This wait usually proved unnervingly anxious as nightmares of having to improvise a rescheduled itinerary that would have me mainlining coffee while making a seemingly endless stream of phone calls from coin-operated public telephones. Let us not forget this was in the pre-cellphone, pre-smartphone, pre-Internet 1980s!

But on this St. Patrick's Day press day, before I could ingest my first java fix in the hotel lobby or even read one section of the *New York Times*, the Malta-born Marc Storace emerged from the elevator *early*—a first! After kissing his young *muse de jour* goodbye, Storace walked over and offered a warm smile and his hand.

"Hi, I'm Marc from Krokus. You must be Alvin from the press office."

"It's an honor to meet you, Marc," I answered while accepting his hand. "Everything O.K. with the flight and the hotel?"

"Everything was great."

"Oh good."

"Can I ask you a question?"

"Sure."

"Where are you from?"

"Born and raised right here in Flushing—out in Queens."

1 . . . 2 . . . 3 . . .

"But where are you *really* from?"

After taking a second to compose myself, I calmly asserted, "Well, I was born here, but my parents are from Canton, in southern China—near Hong Kong."

"Oh, that's great. Have you ever been there?"

"No, I haven't."

"You must go."

"You know . . . I never wanted to go there, but now I think I do."

"Oh, you have to! Have you had breakfast yet?"

"I was going to suggest a place right around the corner."

"Let's go."

With that, the future Last Emperor of Flushing and the reigning first heavy metal–lite frontman of Malta stepped out into the bitterly cold New York March morning. On the first street corner we hit, we bought "Kiss Me, I'm Irish" buttons which we happily wore for the rest of our enjoyable St. Patrick's Day meet-the-press day.

Unlike their namesake, Krokus would not be the first pop-metal flower to break through the frost of the U.S. charts that spring. But on that cold St. Patrick's Day in 1986, their lead singer somehow broke through a different type of decades-long frost. For the first time, I did not have a complete inner and outer meltdown at the inevitable existential question that had plagued me throughout my entire young professional life. Within a year, The Empress Mother and I would proudly make a pilgrimage to where we were *really* from . . . after nearly a quarter-century of living in constant struggle with my ethnicity as part of my longing to belong.

∷

Guilin is a beautiful city. With its picturesque Li River flanked by breathtaking, unusual-looking staccato-layered mountain ranges, one feels as if one is entering an ancient Chinese scroll painting. Water buffalo still roam the riverbanks and, as in so many Chinese scroll paintings, the humans are the smallest figures on the landscape.

On a rain-soaked day in this paradise, our outdoor plans were changed to visit an English-language class. There, our tour group became that day's "lesson." The Empress Mother passed on this activity and rested up back at the hotel. I decided to venture on and was, again, the only Chinese member of the North American tour group.

As soon as I entered the English class, whispers started buzzing around and smiles grew from welcoming to cunning as the teacher introduced her visitors. Finally, a delegation of the tallest boy in the class and a petite pig-tailed girl came forward. If she had been born twenty years earlier, this petite pig-tailed girl would have definitely been a Red Guard. Acting as both his agent and interpreter, the petite pig-tailed girl declared: "He would like to arm wrestle you!"

Taken aback, I sort of uttered, "Well . . . gee . . . I don't know about that."

The petite pig-tailed girl relayed my response in Chinese to her tall comrade. A round of whispers whipped around the room, and a new strategy was whispered into the ear of the petite pig-tailed girl.

"The friendship is first, the match is second," she counter-offered. But her body language was screaming, "Let's get ready to *RUMBUUUUUUUUULLLLLLL!*"

"I don't think that would be a good idea," I politely declined. But the students were just getting started.

"Hey! If there was a war between the United States and China," challenged a boy from the back row, "who would *you* fight for?"

"Yeah, who would *you* fight for?" the class started shouting—more or less in unison. But most aggressively, they were chanting in English.

The teacher finally chastised the students and regained order.

After a long pause in this calm after the storm, I finally said, "I think I'd move to Canada."

In many ways my stateless state had circumnavigated the globe with that incident in the Guilin classroom. I had gone from being one of the few Chinese Americans in Flushing who could not speak fluent Chinese to being one of the few Asians in the New York City music industry—who also did not live in Manhattan—to now being the only Chinese American in a Guilin classroom whose very allegiance, if not ancestry, was being challenged . . . in China.

Still, being asked, "Who would you fight for" in a classroom in China felt akin to being asked, "Which side are you on?" Conversely, being asked, "But where are you *really* from?" at a 1980s NYC music industry function felt like being confronted to confess one's alien identity. It's no wonder that while preparing for the China trip I constantly played the songs "A Sort of Homecoming" by U2 and "Graceland" by Paul Simon—fixating on one Simon lyric in particular: "I've reason to believe we all will be received at Graceland."

On our last day in China, we visited Tiananmen Square, in the heart of the Forbidden City, in the heart of Beijing. Standing in Tiananmen Square, dwarfed by Chairman Mao Zedong's giant portrait, you could feel the spirit of revolution. The same spirit that almost two years later to that day would indelibly etch Tiananmen Square and June 4th onto our collective memory. The same spirit that, thirty-eight years earlier, propelled Chairman Mao Zedong to proclaim the establishment of the People's Republic of China on those same grounds on October 1, 1949.

Like all American "Cold War babies," I was raised to believe that communism was the abject enemy, the evilest of the evil. Back on the predominantly single family–homed, Gentile, suburban-oriented block of The First Flushing Palace, there was this "scary" middle-aged loner of a white guy whom my childhood friends and I called "Mao Zedong." He was our block's Boo Radley or Freddy Krueger and was named, Cold War appropriately, after the Chinese Communist leader. But we weren't even saying it right. At first, I thought we were calling him "Mousey Tongue," like Mickey Mousey Tongue or like some bad deli meat: "Oh, that's 'mousey tongue,' you don't want to eat that."

My friends and I would freeze every time we saw Mousey Tongue. He was a short man who sported a wildly unkempt long, greasy mane of hair and always wore an Army fatigue jacket or pants with combat boots—even during the summer. On our block, everybody said hello to everybody else . . . except for Mousey Tongue. On our block, all of the grown-ups were in hetero relationships. Most of them had children and all of them drove cars. Mousey Tongue was always a loner, always walking, and didn't even own a car. How could he be a grown-up on our block? For years, he marched up and down the block, taking long, rapid, militant strides that resembled stalking more than walking. Sometimes he would march within feet, even inches, of us, without ever saying hello or even making eye contact. In one regard, Mousey Tongue threatened every notion of the block's Eisenhower Americana sense of normalcy. In another strongly felt but unspoken regard, he personified and reinforced the Great American Myth of Rationalization known as the Crazed Lone Gunman. This myth gripped a nation in the guise of Lee Harvey Oswald during the 1960s. In the 1970s' outer boroughs of New York City, this lone gunman myth held us all hostage in the crosshairs of Son of Sam. But, of course, *that* Crazed Lone Gunman was one of *them*. He could never be one of *us*! The fears conjured by this Great American Myth of Rationalization drove me and my childhood friends to regularly ring Mousey Tongue's doorbell and run away. On Halloween, we always threw eggs at his house. But who was really getting tricked?

Mao Zedong's spirit, like his giant portrait, still looms ominously over Tiananmen Square. His body is also there. It lies in state, embalmed in a mausoleum that, to American eyes, looks oddly similar to the Lincoln Memorial. The Empress Mother and I were told that every day, the line of people waiting to pay homage to Mao's embalmed body stretches as far as the eye can see. On our last full day in China, we joined that line and thought of all that Mao had done, good and bad, for his country, his people . . . our world.

As I entered the Mausoleum of Mao Zedong, I started to get goose bumps. The hairs were standing on the back of my neck . . . my heart was pounding . . . my throat grew dry and I lost my breath. When I was finally in the presence of Mao's embalmed body . . . I just stared at his face—illuminated by an eerie lime-green pinpoint spotlight . . . I shivered . . . but all I could think of was: *O.K., that's why we used to call that scary guy on the block Mousey Tongue.*

By calling him Mousey Tongue, we were not imagining this devil to be red in the caricature sense; we were projecting him to be red politically, while being "yellow" militarily—the skin tone of our last three war opponents, Vietnam, Korea, and Japan—and the mid-twentieth-century connotation of being a coward or cheat.

And yes, The Empress Mother's black sneakers were indeed good enough to walk to Beijing.

Chapter 9

:::

The Bigger Picture,
On Screen and Off

AS IF PREORDAINED, on the weekend The Empress Mother and I got back from China, the 1987 Asian American International Film Festival (AAIFF) was opening in Manhattan. It was being held at The Rosemary Theatre, the same Chinatown movie house where my parents used to drag me to see "Pots and Pans movies" on Sunday nights. This was also the same theater where Dad would reconnect with his cronies from the Chinatown Bachelor Society. Now, some sixteen years later, the big screen of The Rosemary no longer flickered with images of Cantonese opera and melodrama. At this film festival, the Chinese American characters spoke good English with their friends, then went home and spoke horrible Chinese with their families. Seeing these characters on the silver screen, I thought, "Wow, I like this. We've come a long way. How can I become part of this?" It felt as if I had finally found an *Our Town* of my own beyond our laundry—a world I could finally feel *and* touch . . . or so I thought.

The following year I joined the staff of Asian CineVision (ACV)—the Chinatown-based media arts and advocacy group that founded and still produces the AAIFF. I was ACV's first full-time publicist and was extremely proud to repurpose my commercial music-biz skills for this essential Asian American community hub. It was an exciting time for Asian American cinema. Wayne Wang's *Chan Is Missing* and *Dim Sum* had received national distribution and acclaim, as had Peter Wang's *A Great Wall* and Steven Okazaki's *Living on Tokyo Time*. In the nonfiction forum, Christine Choy and Renee Tajima's powerful documentary *Who Killed Vincent Chin?* earned an Academy Award nomination.

That same summer I also started my involvement with the then-nascent New York chapter of the Asian American Journalists Association (AAJA). Ironically, it was *Billboard* journalist Brian Chin—whom I was often mistaken for at music industry functions—who passed his invitation on to me . . . so I joined! Through the AAJA, and on the opposite coast, I got to meet an early rock journalism inspiration, Ben Fong-Torres. Ben was one of the original writer/editors of *Rolling Stone* and the only Asian byline I read in the national music media while growing up. Ben was also "immortalized" as a character in Cameron Crowe's Academy Award–winning film *Almost Famous*, which was ostensibly about rock journalism.

I first made contact with Ben through my rock publicity work. At AAJA's 1989 National Convention, held in Ben's hometown of San Francisco, I finally met him in person when he graciously agreed to host an awards ceremony that I was producing for the convention. The day after the ceremony, Ben gave me a tour of his hometown. Naturally, the tour wound up at the corner of Haight & Ashbury. As Ben dropped me off at the intersection that has become heralded as the cradle of the 1967 Summer of Love's counterculture, I asked him:

"How long do you think the '60s will be the barometer for pop culture in this country?"

Pondering this with the experience of someone who was part and parcel of San Francisco's world-changing 1960s counter-culture, Ben replied, "Always."

Getting involved with ACV and the AAJA was a turning point in defining my personal and professional worldview and longing to belong as an adult. Previously, I was able to parlay my rock 'n' roll obsession into becoming a "professional fan" through numerous music publicist appointments and freelance rock journalism assignments. Though that was the greatest life for a rock 'n' roll junky in their late teens to early twenties, by the age of twenty-five I was ready for something else. The eye-opening "sort of homecoming" trip to China further intensified my heartfelt but under-examined longing for a larger landscape. This new world I entered through ACV and the AAJA was the substantial arts/mass media connection my American pop culture psyche needed. This was the connection I thought I had made through the *Kung Fu* television series in the early '70s. By the late '80s, particularly in New York City, many previously disenfranchised groups were getting big-time face time in independent cinema.

This newfound involvement came during the height of late-1980s multiculturalism. In this environ, many African Americans were starting to reclaim and destigmatize the "N word" by using it as an inverted, if aggressive, term of endearment within their community. In this same vein, I thought the time was right to wear my "*juk-sing*-ness," or lack of Old World

Chinese roots, proudly on my sleeve—bolstered, of course, with my tongue firmly in my cheek.

The daily trek to my new Manhattan job was no longer via the 7 train on which I had spent most of my commuter life to date. By the late 1980s, as a result of the direct bond that now existed between "Floo-shing" and Manhattan's Chinatown, there was a new direct bus line between these two communities. Flushing was starting to become NYC's second Chinatown and first Koreatown with more and more of its public signage changing over to Asian characters.

On workday mornings, I got off the Flushing–Chinatown direct bus and headed directly to a Maria's Bakery—this franchise that was so common in Chinese neighborhoods. Maria's looks like a Dunkin' Donuts except that the shelves were stocked with exquisite-looking sweets that, at least to the American palate, were not quite as sweet on the tongue as they were on the eye. My first attempts to order coffee in Chinese were met with alternately amused and dismissive whispers of *Juk-Sing*. To their surprise, I responded to their whispers with a robust "Yes! '*Juk-Sing*,' that's me!"—completely owning my lack of China or even Chinatown roots without backing down. A ritual was born. My twice-a-day Maria's Bakery coffee stops became the highlight of the employees' day and mine—with the entire staff joyously shouting, "Ha-low *Juk-Sing*," or "*Juk-Sing* is here!" upon my arrival.

After Maria's, it was up the four flights of shaky old wooden stairs that bordered uncomfortably close to being a fire hazard to ACV's office at 32 East Broadway. As I joyously scaled each challenging step up toward a new world of wonder that was ACV, I felt as if I were gleefully cavorting with the spirits of the Lower East Side—particularly the silenced voices of huddled, sweatshop-working masses and bohemians past. Although this, too, became a community I could feel but not touch, this one somehow felt more compatible. Comfortable, even.

This level of comfort was markedly different from the way I felt on some of my first visits to Chinatown relatives' homes in similar early-twentieth-century buildings in the 1970s. As a young child on the Chinatown streets, I could at least pass myself off as a local. But once inside those Chinatown tenement apartments, I reverted to my cowering Last Emperor Pu Yi/*Tommy* propensity. I began to understand just how far Flushing was from Chinatown and The City during that time.

Exiting the somewhat familiar Chinatown streets and entering the dimly lit, narrow hallways of those tenement buildings of my relatives, I felt like I was embarking on a cultural excavation—only this society was living, even if I, at times, lost my breath in its presence. One day, my pampered outer borough nervous system broke down and I had a good old-fashioned meltdown from my inability to adapt to these perceived challenging environs.

"I don't want to sit. I don't want to eat. I just want to go home," I intoned to no one in particular, then just stood and stewed alone in the corner.

"*Fee doy fonna kee ah?*" ["Chubby boy wants to go home huh?"] The Empress Mother's hosts good-naturedly offered with loud, stinging laughter.

"*Be-be mutt do uhm hue,*" ["He's the baby of the family, he doesn't know anything."] The Empress Mother would apologize with embarrassment.

"*Koy na may-guk chut-sigh; juk-sing,*" ["These American-born Chinese today are like hollow bamboo,"] another of The

Empress Mother's hosts would add, igniting loud bursts of laughter.

By 1988, The Empress Mother's *juk-sing* son was finally proud and prepared to embrace everything that Chinatown had to offer. For Mother's Day of that year, I treated The Empress Mother to a matinee Cantonese opera performance at the Sun Sing Theater—literally beneath the Manhattan Bridge on East Broadway. Vertical subtitles in Chinese bridged both the Cantonese- and Mandarin-speaking and reading members of the audience. As a nonspeaker and nonreader of Chinese, I remember greatly admiring the music, movement, and dance. Sadly, the Sun Sing Theater is now a Hong Kong–style mall.

The 1988 Asian American International Film Festival turned out to be the last one to be presented at The Rosemary Theatre in Chinatown. Proudly, ACV's final film festival in Chinatown would garner the largest audience to date for that well-deserving event. Our unprecedented attendance numbers were also greatly assisted by The Rosemary Theatre's old school/Old World box office policy. In that venue, a hot film had no cap on the amount of tickets that could be sold (or corresponding number of audience members sitting in the aisles, standing by the exit signs, etc.). The Rosemary management maintained a box office policy that was the equivalent of ACV's well-worn wooden stairs—a potential fire hazard.

The Rosemary's box office was a pane of gold-tinted one-way glass, presumably bulletproof, with a small slot on the bottom through which filmgoers placed their money and received their tickets. As you gazed at your own gold-tinted reflection and listened to the disembodied Cantonese-inflected voice, the box office seemed more like a portal to an alternate universe than a venerable old Chinatown movie house.

⋮

On the final day of the 1988 AAIFF, as the sun was shining brightly on The Rosemary Theatre at the foot of the Manhattan Bridge—now the departure point for many a discount Chinatown commuter bus—I was coordinating the ticket holder's line when all of a sudden the spirit moved me . . . it felt as if all of the stars in the multicultural cosmos were aligning and I was in the zone. The moment had finally arrived to cross the final frontier: speaking the mother tongue . . . kind of like when TV *Kung Fu* master Kwai Chang Caine was ready to snatch that pebble from his master's hand . . . or when Tommy was ready to smash that mirror that held him inside his "see me, feel me" mode . . . but fiction is fiction and real life is, well . . . at any rate (and through any metaphor) there was no doubt that I was feeling my Asian American oats!

During the festival's final Saturday matinee, as I formed the ticket holder's line, I loudly and proudly announced: "*Nee you fee, kee oh koy*"—simply trying to say, "Ticket holders please, form a line here."

People just looked at me with bewilderment.

"*Nee you fee, kee oh koy,*" I announced even louder, if a little less prouder.

The looks of bewilderment turned ugly, then to outright scorn.

From behind me I heard a loud burst of laughter from my Hong Kong–born supervisor. He walked over and in perfect Cantonese explained to the crowd that I was mispronouncing the inflection of "ticket" so badly that it was coming out as "fat." So, instead of saying, "Ticket holders please, form a line here," I was saying, "Fat people: Get over there!"

Everyone just laughed, shook their heads, and lamented, "*Juk-Sing*." Hollow bamboo. But this was no late-'80s multicultural act of inverted multicultural endearment in the vein of my self-effacing exchanges with the staff at Maria's Bakery. This "*juk-sing*" stung. The ticket holders meant, "Hollow bamboo . . . Dead wood" in its oldest school connotation to again point out that I still was really not one of them. As things go in China, so go things in Chinatown.

A few months after that last AAIFF in Chinatown, the epic film *The Last Emperor* was given an Oscar-contender's holiday weekend release. I took The Empress Mother. I thought, maybe seeing a Chinese story in a movie theater outside of Chinatown might have the same power for her as first seeing Asian American cinema had for me.

There we were: watching a Hollywood epic about the last feudal leader of our ancestral homeland, in a movie directed by an Italian filmmaker. During the first few scenes, The Empress Mother kept asking why everyone in The Forbidden City was speaking English. Eventually, she suspended her disbelief and settled in for the surreal ride that is Hollywood. Soon, we were even *ooh*-ing and *aah*-ing at the Beijing sights we had seen the summer before. Then came *the scene*. It's 1967. Pu Yi is now a common citizen. He has been thrice removed from his emperorship by the Nationalist, Communist, and Cultural Revolutions. Citizen Pu Yi purchases a ticket to gain entry to The Forbidden City that was his childhood palace.

As the elderly former emperor struggles to walk up those same steps that he used to bound up effortlessly as a child, The Empress Mother and I both begin to weep. For a moment we are back at the Sunday night "Pots and Pans movies" in Chinatown. Only this time it was just the two of us. Dad was no longer sitting next to us surrounded by the last generation of Chinatown Bachelor Society survivors. And this time I was finally seeing the bigger picture—on screen and off.

Chapter 10

Trip the Light,
Gorgeous Mosaic

Double Happiness, Discovering
Playwriting and Activism

(1st verse) Lose that shit this ain't the Mainland
I'm the Goong Hay Kid, hope you understand:
Don't do no kowtowing or no rickshaw.
So don't be talking no dragons or the Great Wall.
I ain't good in math, don't know kung fu.
Ditto for Confucius or Fu Manchu.
So don't mess with me or call me Bruce Lee.
'Cause ain't no one badder than Kid Goong Hay
CHORUS: Rock Me Goong Hay! (four times)
. . . (Last Verse) Yellow fever was our lot in this country
Now we're the so-called "model minority"
Which really don't mean shit, if you think about it
'Cause plenty still despise our slanty eyes
Don't overcompensate for your sorry state
You can't keep us in the laundry or the railroad track
'CAUSE IT TAKES A NATION OF BILLIONS . . . TO
*   HOLD US PEOPLE BACK!*

"Rock Me Gung Hay!" from *THE GOONG HAY KID*

"Ngen-sang ngooy-mong"	*(People's lives are like dreams . . .)*
"Ngen-ting ngooy-seu"	*(Human nature has no taste— like water . . .)*
"Ngen-sang sigh seng"	*(People in this world . . .)*
"Tong-kee haw-see"	*(How long do we have . . .)*
"Ngen-ting slee-gee"	*(People's natures are like paper . . .)*
"Jeng jeng buck"	*(Every sheet is thin . . .)*
"Sly-see gneu-key"	*(What we know is strange . . .)*
"Guk guk sleng"	*('Cause everything is new . . .)*

"People's Lives Are Like Dreams" traditional
Cantonese lullaby Included in *THE GOONG HAY KID*

These two lyrics bookend my punk-rap play with songs, *The Goong Hay Kid*. "Rock Me Goong Hay" is the show's finale. It is an homage to Public Enemy's "Fight the Power" and *Do the Right Thing*—the 1989 Spike Lee "joint" in which the song ignites the opening credits along with some spectacular raw, wild-style dancing from Rosie Perez. "People's Lives Are Like Dreams," the play's prologue and epilogue, is a traditional Cantonese lullaby that The Empress Mother used to sing around our laundry and in both Flushing Palaces of The Eng Dynasty. These two lyrics also represent the contours of my disposition during the late 1980s/early '90s multiculturalism movement. A common culinary analogy was that through multiculturalism, the proverbial melting pot of America was now becoming a mixed salad . . . we were all still in the same bowl but no longer required to be reduced to our homogenized lowest common denominators. In other words, we were finally free to fully embrace our ethnically, racially, and culturally diverse selves as well as any and all sexual preferences. In New York City, this era was famously celebrated as "The Gorgeous Mosaic" by our first black mayor, the late Honorable David N. Dinkins. The election of Dinkins was in 1989. It would take until 2021 for the election of New York City's second black mayor, Eric Adams. The Gorgeous Mosaic era redefined the American frame through which I had been longing to belong to my entire life as well as my outlook onto the world at large and in Flushing in particular.

During this time, Flushing was also going through a major "Gorgeous Mosaic" makeover. After the late 1970s NYC economic downturn, Flushing had become a compromised ghost of its old self—not unlike the ones with the shuttered, boarded-up businesses that haunt a well-known Bruce Springsteen song of that era, "My Hometown." It would take another change in U.S. immigration policy to help bolster not just the Chinese community but also communities like Flushing that were hit hard by the economic slump throughout America.

In 1979, the Democratic administration of President Jimmy Carter formally recognized the Communist government of the People's Republic of China. As a result, the PRC was granted its own U.S. immigration quota and no longer had to share the "Chinese quota" with Hong Kong and Taiwan. To ride this rising tide, Flushing officials struck a deal with a few Chinese developers to stimulate growth, and grow Flushing did—flourishing with a constant influx of new PRC–HK–Taiwan immigrants finding their way to revive and reinvent my hometown.

Along with this virtually overnight exponential growth of Asian immigrants, Chinese-language signs started dominating the Flushing landscape. As a result, I was officially part of a growing new minority: one of the few American Born Chinese (ABCs) in the neighborhood who did not speak fluent Mandarin—now the official Chinese language—and was only minimally convincing in our family's Toisan dialect of Cantonese.

Things were changing all over—rapidly and unexpectedly. Like all changes, they are not detours or obstacles. These changes are the path. It was in the midst of all of this that I made a major life change.

███

The number 8 holds special significance for the Chinese. It is a homonym of good fortune and a symbol of good luck and long life. Thus, 1988 portended to be a good year to start new things as well as to renew older ones. It was also The Year of the Dragon. Traditionally, the dragon symbolizes power, nobleness, honor, luck, and success. Alongside making the transition from the music biz to Director of Public Relations for Asian CineVision (ACV) and discovering New York City's Asian American arts and activism world, I was also looking to rekindle dormant creative pursuits—the last of which were performing and songwriting forays with teenage punk rock bands. One of my first tasks and public events at ACV was to assist writer/performance artist Jessica Hagedorn and critic/curator Daryl Chin with their acclaimed literary series, "Talk N Cheap." The series' first guest of 1988 was playwright David Henry Hwang. He was to read from M. Butterfly, the play that would make his Broadway debut the following month. The ACV "Talk N Cheap" reading was the first NYC public reading from M. Butterfly.

As Hwang read startling passages from his play that would soon redefine the parameters of artistic explorations of East–West sociosexual political relations, I was buzzing with a feeling I had not known since first hearing The Who's Tommy or David Johansen's "Funky But Chic." As culturally sheltered as this may sound, it wasn't until the age of twenty-five that something besides rock 'n' roll had as much of a primal and intellectual impact.

For those of us fortunate enough to be in the room that night for its first NYC public reading, as well as for those of us who worked in the Asian American arts and activism communities, M. Butterfly became one of those seminal works that redefined our world into before and after. David Henry Hwang's powerful play proved that there was a place for our voices and visions on the biggest theatrical stage in New York City and the world. *M. Butterfly* would go on to have a celebrated extended run on Broadway—winning the 1988 Tony Award for Best Play, as well as a Best Actor Tony Award for its star, B. D. Wong. As of this writing, Hwang and Wong are still the only Asian American theatre artists to win Tony Awards. The morning after that provocative first public reading from *M. Butterfly*, I decided to apply for a playwriting workshop instead of the screenwriting workshop I had been strongly considering at "The Writer's Voice"—the creative writing program of the 63rd Street YMCA on the Upper West Side.

While I had long longed to see myself, and my community's concerns, on the small screen of television as well as on the silver screen of cinema, my growing up in Flushing, Queens, in an immigrant Chinese household in which only one parent spoke fluent English meant that Broadway and theatre could not have been more remote. Yet less than a year after a worldview-changing trip that The Empress Mother and I made to China, I took the first steps in a most roundabout journey to devoting my professional life to theatre and playwriting. The more I thought about playwriting, the more I found this form to mirror what I loved about rock 'n' roll and, most distinctly, what I revered in rock 'n' roll songwriters. Both the playwriting and songwriting processes alternate between the solitude of artistic inquiry as a writer that leads to the collaborative process of creating live performance. Plays are also like songs in that they can be reinterpreted in endless styles, idioms, or genres for productions. At the end of the day, playwrights and song-writers are also witnesses to and portraitists of history. As I was always equally captivated by the cathartic performative power of rock 'n' roll, gravitating to theatre was also like diving into the sea from which the river of rock 'n' roll flows.

A few days after seeing one of the first M. Butterfly preview performances on Broadway, I was accepted into the playwriting workshop at The Writer's Voice. A few weeks later, still buoyed by the zeitgeist confirmation of M. Butterfly's fast becoming a barrier-breaking, history-making Broadway hit, I floated up the stairs, through the swimming pool–chlorinated air of the 63rd Street YMCA, to my first playwriting class at The Writer's Voice. It was a magical time for a Chinese American to begin his journey as a playwright.

That first day of class, I sat next to a fellow playwriting traveler, Peter Brightbill, who would become a lifelong friend and through whom I would eventually meet my wife, Wendy Wasdahl. Our first playwriting teacher and one of the most important teachers in my life was Lavonne Mueller. I studied with her for several years at The Writer's Voice. Now, as I was starting to navigate this new road as a playwright, the longing to belong evolved into seizing the opportunity to define community and culture on my own terms and through my own words, rather than seeking other artists to define and articulate my identity. Still, the need to speak to the various communities with which one has always traveled was important. This need was coupled with the constructive competitiveness of a classroom and first assignments.

To tackle the first assignment in my first playwriting workshop course at The Writer's Voice, I revisited a performance art project from a year earlier. For a "Comedy Night" benefit for the New York chapter of the Asian American Journalists Association (AAJA), I had written and produced a ten-minute slide show that served as a prelude to a "faux reunion concert" of an imaginary Chinese rock 'n' roll band, "Big Character Poster" (BCP). The slide show itself was developed at open mic nights at Dixon

Place when it was still situated in founding director Ellie Covan's East 1st Street living room. It should also be noted that the AAJA benefit was produced by the late Asian American "photographer laureate" and force-of-nature activist Corky Lee, while the actual BCP slide photography was by Bethany Jacobson, who has since gone on to distinguish herself as a filmmaker and educator. The benefit was held at the revered Jazz Coalition run by another NYC Asian American legend, Cobi Narita.

In BCP's fictitious life, the band was supposedly reuniting for the first time since 1968—twenty years before. The result was a multimedia "mini-mockumentary" for the stage entitled *The 20th Anniversary Reunion Concert of Big Character Poster.* With this 1988 project I attempted to merge my lifelong rock 'n' roll passion with my newfound Chinese American pride and activism—as well as pay homage to the transformative activist power of a different year that ended in 8—that of the revolutionary 1968 . . . and life would soon imitate art.

The project's premise focused on a fictitious Chinese rock band comprising grizzled veterans of both the 1960s' Cultural Revolution of the People's Republic of China and the American pop culture "revolution." They started out in the early 1960s as the Tiananmen Square house band, "The Tiananmen Squares." During the late-'60s' Cultural Revolution, they were sentenced to playing only "dirty Western pop music" and rebranded "Big Character Poster." Naturally this strategy backfired, and the band became a subversive, international underground phenomenon.

Actual "big character posters" were how Cultural Revolution dissidents communicated. They hastily pasted their poster manifestos on walls where other dissidents could copy the message before government authorities and soldiers would tear down these "counter-revolutionary" communiqués. In my idealistic worldview, this "good bad subversive news" would be communicated through rock 'n' roll . . . and now playwriting, performance art, and theatre.

▚▚

Off-stage, the singular purpose of this entire venture was to get to know a Chinese American filmmaker who had strongly influenced the post-punk early-twenties years of my high school best friend, Ray Wong, and me. During that time—the mid-1980s—Asian American filmmakers such as Wayne Wang and Peter Wang (no relation) were starting to receive national recognition. Wayne was born and raised in Hong Kong, Peter in Taiwan. Their respective breakthrough films, *Chan Is Missing* (1982) and *A Great Wall* (1986), primarily utilized talent from the San Francisco Bay Area Asian American acting and theatre communities. Between these films, Steve Ning's *Freckled Rice* was released independently. *Freckled Rice* centers on a ten-year-old Chinese American boy's coming of age in Boston's Chinatown during the 1960s. Like Ray and me, Steve Ning was an East Coast American-born Chinese "*juk-sing.*" His film utilized a primarily NYC- and East Coast–based cast, crew, and creative team. While I could deeply feel parts of myself in Wayne Wang's and Peter Wang's films, with Ning and *Freckled Rice*'s East Coast and ABC/*juk-sing* sensibilities, I could feel *and see* all of myself for the first time on the silver screen. The ten-year-old protagonist even had an older brother who was in a rock band!

Ray and I first met Steve when we shamelessly dominated a post-screening question-and-answer session with a *Freckled Rice* audience in 1985. A few years later, I started seeing Steve at ACV and Asian American arts and advocacy events . . . and an idea was born. This idea so excited me that I called Ray from a pay phone booth during a break from a planning meeting for the AAJA "Comedy Night" benefit. (This was way before cellphones . . . when even flip phones were still seen solely as futuristic creations from *Star Trek*.)

"Ray, there's an opportunity to get back on stage!" I shouted to his stunned silence.

"Steve Ning, 'that *Freckled Rice* guy,' runs in these circles and I'm sure he must play an instrument," I rattled off at a breakneck pace . . . no response from Ray.

"Why don't we see if he does and if he'd like to take part in a fake comedy–performance art, all-Chinese rock band for this AAJA benefit?"

Ray was still speechless.

"Look, even if the project goes nowhere, maybe we'll get to know that '*Freckled Rice* guy.'"

On the other end, there was still silence. In my frenzy, I took Ray's silence to be a yes.

▮▮▮

After the AAJA planning meeting, a group of us went to the opening of an exhibit at the Chinatown History Project, now known as the Museum of Chinese in the Americas, and there was Steve Ning. I politely reintroduced myself as one of the two guys who had pestered him after a screening two years before. Not surprisingly, he remembered Ray and me. After some pleasantries, I got down to business.

"Do you, as *Freckled Rice* implies, play an instrument?" I breathlessly asked.

Steve's face broke into a warm and beatific smile, and he nodded his head yes.

"Would you be interested in taking part in a fake comedy–performance art, all-Chinese rock band for this AAJA benefit?"

I asked, feeling as nervous as a teenager asking a girl out for the first time.

Steve just softly replied, "Yeah, I play the bass and it sounds like fun."

I could feel that the combination of my mania and his manners would be a winning combination. I felt like I'd just secured my dream date, and in many ways I had. With Steve Ning on board, our faux all-Asian rock band was ready to roll at the AAJA Comedy Night benefit. I finally found a vehicle to merge my disparate worlds of rock 'n' roll and Asian American fervor with my dormant desire to write and create. And just like with our cover band, The Grips, back in Flushing High School, and in classic punk rock/garage band DIY fashion, Ray and I secured the gig first and *then* put the band together.

At the AAJA Comedy Night benefit, the ten-minute "mockumentary" slide show that comically chronicled our "saga" as a prelude to our grand "reunion" performance garnered a rousing response. Then . . . the audience had a significantly less enthusiastic reaction to our "musical" performance—actually warmed-up servings from a leftover set list of cover songs from my high school band, The Grips. From then on, I knew that my main instrument was the typewriter and not the guitar. Still, this project was a crucial first step in my journey from the sidelines of music promotion and back onto the stage—literally—of creating art. For my first assignments in The Writer's Voice playwriting course, I developed that ten-minute slide show into a one-act play. A year later, ". . . *Big Character Poster*" was given a three-night workshop production with the Medicine Show Theatre Ensemble—founded by two alums of Joseph Chaikin's seminal Open Theatre, Barbara Vann and James Barbosa. I even got to perform one of the roles alongside future Obie Award winner Jojo Gonzalez, among others.

■■■

Around this time, I also started exploring how the post–punk/ rock 'n' roll aesthetic was informing other mediums. In alternative-performance spaces throughout Lower Manhattan like La MaMa, e.t.c., Dixon Place, Gusto House, Franklin Furnace, and Performance Space 122 (P.S. 122), I started taking in performances from the likes of Split Britches, Urban Bush Women, Ping Chong & Company, and the "Teenytown" trio comprising Laurie Carlos, Robbie McCauley, and my ACV colleague Jessica Hagedorn. I also became a frequent attendee of the Brooklyn Academy of Music (BAM). At BAM, I was lucky to see and be spellbound by such game-changing works as Laurie Anderson's two-night epic *United States, Parts I–IV*; the Squat Theatre's *L Train to Eldorado;* and the second New York City production of Philip Glass and Robert Wilson's groundbreaking opera *Einstein on the Beach.* During that remarkable stars-aligning period following my first trip to China, the John Adams and Alice Goodman opera *Nixon in China* also had its New York premiere at BAM's Next Wave Festival.

As an avid believer in the punk DIY ethos and a lifelong admirer of singer/songwriters—solo and as bandleaders—I was particularly intrigued by the solo performers of that era. This newer generation of theatre and performance artists taught me that there were forms and audiences for raw, raucous artistic inquiry and social dialogue beyond the realm of a three- or four-minute song. Some of these solo performers included the aforementioned Laurie Anderson, as well as Spalding Gray, Penny Arcade, Eric Bogosian, Holly Hughes, Frank Maya, and Ethyl Eichelberger—the last three of these also had a profound personal impact. All of these artists, solo and ensemble, were also redefining how identity politics was being refined and defined on the stages, streets, and even in the U.S. Supreme Court of this "Gorgeous Mosaic" era.

Perhaps the most singular "downtown" solo performer of that or any era was Ethyl Eichelberger. An alum of the Ridiculous Theatrical Company and Trinity Rep in Providence, she was a six-foot-plus drag queen who cavorted around in enormous high heels—usually while playing an accordion. Her classical training as an actor, playwright, singer, and instrumentalist, combined with her indomitable on-stage presence, energy, and subversive wit, made Ethyl a peerless performer. With every performance, she was challenging and shattering so-called uptown and downtown standards and aesthetics of theatre—as well as being. Many a show culminated with her performing outrageous and grandiose cartwheels in often hole-in-the-wall venues that could barely contain her body or spirit. While I greatly admired Ethyl's virtuosity, as I was an untrained actor and nascent playwright, I knew that my journey into the performance/theatre world would have to take a very different path. From the start I paid close, analytic attention to solo performers whom I characterized as writers first and performers second, such as Frank Maya and Holly Hughes.

Before he became renowned in the early '90s as one of the first openly gay stand-up comics, Frank Maya was a radiant presence on the late '80s downtown performance art scene. He captured the pulse of intergenerational and family dilemmas of the gay community with a warmer, comic touch—tossing out observations such as "my father asked me if [then–New York City Mayor Ed] Koch is gay—as if we have a list or something." This warmer touch, along with his oft-discussed desires for commercial mainstream success, was often at odds with the decidedly "no-sell-out/under-the-radar proud" downtown ethos. Like Ethyl Eichelberger, Frank Maya was also challenging and shattering the parameters of two divergent—some might even say polarized—theatre communities: stand-up comics and performance artists. My first "non–rock 'n' roll" journalistic work explored this "stand-up comic vs. performance artist" chasm. For this article I had the opportunity to interview both Maya and Reno—another stellar downtown solo performer. The piece was published in the short-lived *P.S. 122 Newsletter*—an outreach arm of the "P.T.A.," a collective of P.S. 122's friends and followers. This P.T.A. was founded by P.S. 122's then–Development Director, Alan Siege, who became a lifelong friend and at whose home I would later meet my wife.

Where Maya had a mainstream-ish, comic sheen to his work, Holly Hughes was an unapologetic militant feminist lesbian sensuous provocateur.

So there's this guy at work, right. Jeez! Always hovering over my PC asking me if I want to go to a Blarney Stone, right? So finally I said to him: "Look, I hate you. You're an idiot. I'm a lesbian. You touch me, you're a dead man, okay?"

or

Where are all the great women artists? Is that a question for me? You know where they are—they're out in the kitchen, for chrissakes, making you a fucking cup of coffee, okay?

These were both from a solo performance/spoken-word piece, *World Without End*—a piece I saw many times. Soon, Hughes would be waging these social/culture wars in the U.S. Supreme Court as part of a very different "Gang of Four" known as the "NEA 4"—that also included performance artists Karen Finley, John Fleck, and Tim Miller.

In 1990, these four artists had their National Endowment for the Arts solo performance grants rescinded by then–NEA Chairman John Frohnmayer. The decision was based on pressure from the Republican administration of then-President George H. W. Bush (whom Rachel Maddow refers to as "Poppy Bush") to adhere to the "Decency Clause." This clause was designed as an alternative to (but hardly an undoing of) the so-called Helms Amendment of 1989, created by notorious Republican Senator Jesse Helms. This clause and amendment prohibited the NEA from funding "obscene or indecent materials, including but not limited to depictions of sadomasochism, homoeroticism, the exploitation of children, or individuals engaged in sex acts."

The "NEA 4" sued the federal government in early 1991 to have their grants reinstated as well as to challenge the constitutionality of the Decency Clause. They won twice on having their grants reinstated—proving victorious in both the initial lawsuit and its appeal. But they were not victorious in their efforts to overturn the constitutionality of the Decency Clause. Hughes, Finley, Fleck, and Miller eventually wound up accepting out-of-court cash settlements from the government. On stage, Hughes responded with two performance pieces, *Clit Notes* and *Preaching to the Perverted*, in which she riffed on and dramatized the legal and cultural proceedings.

The "NEA 4" episode and overall political climate had a direct impact on my first full-length solo performance work, *Over the Counter Culture*, performed in Franklin Furnace's 1991 "In Exile" series at the historic Judson Memorial Church—long revered as a cradle of downtown NYC resistance and experimentation.

Franklin Furnace, a venerable downtown performance space and art gallery founded by Martha Wilson (and now a digital archive of all things experimental performance, text, and visual art), was in exile from its own persecution that was a direct result of pressure from the aforementioned Senator Helms. This pressure put into motion audits by both the Internal Revenue Service and the State Comptroller of New York, as well as the New York City Fire Department's closing down Franklin

Furnace as an "illegal social club." To save their 1991 Spring Performance Series, Judson Memorial Church housed Franklin Furnace "In Exile."

Over the Counter Culture was presented in this series in April 1991. The work is an episodic collage of multimedia monologues, recorded spoken-word pieces set to slides (yes, slides), as well as songs performed live with my music/audio collaborator, Timothy Cramer. All of the pieces addressed the conflict between the "Gorgeous Mosaic" multiculturalism being cultivated and celebrated in New York City and the national climate of post–Gulf War "shock and awe" of that one-month earthquake of a war. Aftershocks from that war are still being felt like tremors—from the concerted conservative crackdown on alternative and counterculture arts and lifestyles by the likes of Senator Helms as well as the commercial co-opting and diluting of these same viewpoints that is just as dangerous and subversive. The work also did not include any overt Asian American themes or characters—yet by virtue of its authorship I still presented the work as Asian American performance art and theatre under the overall umbrella of NYC Art. For me, this is also part and parcel of "Gorgeous Mosaic" representation—the artistic freedom to not stay in my "ethnic lane" and create only works that contain overtly Asian American "themes" and characters.

For *Over the Counter Culture* as well as a ten-minute performance in P.S. 122's "Avant-Garde-Arama"—then under the stellar direction of performance artist Salley May—I got to work with Kate Stafford, the director of Holly Hughes's *World Without End*, which had greatly influenced me. Our collaboration was a result of P.S. 122's "CON Artists" program (it stood for "Consultant Artists"). This was an innovative program created by Mark Russell, P.S. 122's Artistic Director, that provided funding for artists to *Con*-nect with each other to create new work. Through our collaboration, I learned that Kate was also the primary director of the Five Lesbian Brothers ensemble— through which we had unexpected common ground. This ensemble included Lisa Kron, who would make history twice—as the first downtown performance artist to have her show on Broadway with *Well* in 2006 and then being a Tony Award winner from the first all-female creative team for the musical adaptation of Alison Bechdel's graphic memoir *Fun Home*. Kron's partner at that time, Peg Healey, also one of the Five Lesbian Brothers, hailed from Queens. My brother Herman played bass in The Peggy Healey Band. For the Five Lesbian Brothers and forward, she was known professionally as Peg Healey. Through my collaboration and conversations with Kate Stafford, I learned as much about representation and identity politics on the stage as I did from *M. Butterfly*.

Overall, I was aglow from this newfound world of expression and activism on-stage and off. In this new light, I also found myself in an old familiar shadow. My love of the downtown solo/performance world put me in another quandary of sorts between conventional "uptown" plot-/narrative-driven theatre like *M. Butterfly* and more experimental, episodic "downtown" theatre and performance art like *World Without End*. It was no longer just a matter of which way to turn in order to curry favor with dominating neighborhood cliques in my ongoing battle of longing to belong. Now, rather than feeling the pressure to choose one over the other, I was slowly gravitating to the more inclusive view that I comprised all of the above and no longer none of the above. A journey that is still evolving.

Also like the DIY punk scene, I found the downtown solo/performance art world to be much more approachable off-stage than the "traditional/mainstream uptown" theatre artists. These glimpses into their personal lives also informed how I interpreted their work on stage. Thus, more than three decades later, I still remember the sight of Ethyl Eichelberger after the show. Following the cartwheeling, virtuoso accordion playing, and punk/shaman/Shakespearean odes and manic opera/musical theatre anti-etudes, Ethyl would load her plentiful props, costumes, and accordion into a supermarket shopping cart. Then, she would slowly wheel the full cart through the streets of Lower Manhattan. With all due respect to her singular performances, this is my most poignant and enduring image and impression of the late, great Ethyl Eichelberger . . . art, love, and life all rolled into one cart, bumpily navigating the unevenly paved streets under the harsh streetlights of Lower Manhattan.

Tragically, those streets would get emptier and emptier within a few short years as the AIDS epidemic ended the lives of Ethyl Eichelberger, Frank Maya, and way too many other souls of our city and arts world. Though AIDS was first identified in the early 1980s, it would take until the early-'90s high-profile passing of Queen's lead singer, Freddie Mercury, and the HIV diagnosis of NBA basketball legend Magic Johnson to have AIDS acknowledged as a dire global epidemic. As a teenager I had painted my fingernails black in emulation of Freddie Mercury. As a lifelong basketball fan, I had greatly admired Magic Johnson. It was a tragedy in and of itself that it took this "high-profile" casualty and diagnosis to enter a broader general conversation on AIDS. To quote Reverend Al Sharpton's reaction to the Rodney King verdict, another tipping point of this era, in which only two of the four officers who were caught on videotape viciously beating the L.A. motorist in a flagrant show of police brutality were found guilty: "It's half of what we wanted but twice as much as we've ever had."

Literally on the other side of the world, in The People's Republic of China (PRC), the Pro-Democracy movement was amplifying its calls to action into a full-throated roar. During the spring of 1989, the Pro-Democracy student activists timed their demonstrations to coincide with a Beijing visit from then–Soviet Union leader Mikhail Gorbachev—still aglow from the worldwide embracing of his *glasnost* reformations. The Chinese students wanted to grab some of that glow for themselves and took to voicing their declarations for democracy to a worldwide audience . . . from Tiananmen Square! As implausible as it seemed, the Pro-Democracy students had taken over the very same hallowed ground from which Mao Zedong had declared the founding of the PRC almost forty years before, the same square where the Chairman's imposing portrait still looms. Soon after this triumph, the ranks of the students and youth swelled to also include workers. The momentum of the movement even made the soldiers pull back from their usual perfunctory crackdown by force. And for a brief time and logic-defying weeks, it looked as if the Communist–Socialist utopia of the unification of "Worker-Peasant-Soldier-Student" was being realized and sustained by China's 1989 Pro-Democracy movement!

It was against this sociopolitical backdrop that an old Flushing High School friend, Melissa Cahill, expressed interest in adapting my *Big Character Poster* play for her B.A. thesis project in film production at Hunter College. When this adaptation process started in late 1988, I had to explain many of the 1968 Cultural Revolution references at all of our developmental workshops and script sessions. A few short months later, China's Pro-Democracy student/youth movement of 1989 made all of *Big Character Poster*'s heretofore obscure Cultural Revolution references such as "Tiananmen Square" household names. With equipment and crew from the Hunter College film program and a grant from Apparatus Films—a group comprising Todd Haynes, Christine Vachon, and Barry Elsworth—the short film was completed. The cast featured the band that had actually played at the AAJA comedy benefit—including

Steve Ning, Ray, and me. Sadly, Steve passed away before the film was completed, but not before he had inspired a new generation of "*juk-sings*."

On an almost daily basis, the broadcast news coverage of the movement's occupation of Tiananmen Square mirrored the archival footage from the 1968 Cultural Revolution that Melissa was masterfully cutting in to our film. In another "life imitates art" occurrence, China's Pro-Democracy movement also cultivated its first rock star spokesperson, Cui Jian. In May 1989, I wrote a feature article on Cui Jian in the *Village Voice* entitled "Rock Star Over China."

For the first and, sadly, only time I could remember, the voice and contemporary struggle of China and Chinese people the world over were the focus of the entire world. After growing up with almost all things Chinese being dismissed, even disdained, under the post–Cold War cloud of China's being Communist Public Enemy #2, this was a shocking and most welcome change. Still also floating on a cultural Cloud 9 from a first visit to China, and overall awakening and acceptance of my ethnicity, the Pro-Democracy movement had me rising to an even higher plane . . . for a few short weeks.

On June 4, 1989, the Pro-Democracy movement came to a bloody demise as Chinese Army tanks rolled into Tiananmen Square—literally crushing the movement. In the end, the death toll of the June 4th crackdown was estimated to be close to 10,000, with many more injured.

On an unusually cold, windy, and rainy June afternoon, I joined thousands of New Yorkers who took to our city's streets to mourn and pledge our solidarity to the fallen Pro-Democracy martyrs, as well as to continue the resistance that they had started. Some marchers even created a replica of the "Goddess of Democracy." This was the 33-foot papier-mâché sculpture that was crafted by the students and became an icon in all Tiananmen Square imagery of this uprising. The sculpture channeled both the Statue of Liberty and *Worker and Kolkhoz Woman*. The latter was a Vera Mukhina stainless-steel Art Deco sculpture of two figures with a sickle and hammer raised over their heads. This sculpture was created for the Soviet Pavilion of the 1937 World's Fair in Paris and was later moved to a public square of the Russian Exhibition Centre in Moscow. The Goddess of Democracy held a torch of liberty aloft with both hands.

We gathered at the United Nations on the East Side of Manhattan and marched westward to the Chinese Consulate. Under frequent heavy downpours, we received cheers, shouts of solidarity, and the raising of peace signs and power fists. These gestures of solidarity came from people on the streets, as well as from many more crammed onto balconies or around office windows. Marchers and allies seemed to be asking the same existential question that protest marchers had been asking twenty years earlier—the same one they would still be asking some twenty or thirty years later: "Who'll stop the rain" . . . of oppression . . . suppression . . . spiritual and cultural extermination?

Standing in the pouring rain outside the Chinese Consulate, I remembered The Empress Mother's always saying that when it rained on Mother's Day it was because all the mothers of the world were crying. The tears of rain soaking our eyes and streets at that march represented all the distraught souls and devastated dreams of the workers, peasants, soldiers, and, most of all, the brave students who embodied and propelled China's Pro-Democracy movement—along with those they had inspired around the world. I also flashed back to being taken to the 1960s' Civil Rights–era Asian American protests by my brother

Victor and his first wife, Judy. At these rallies, we often saw the Asian American folk-rock trio Yellow Pearl. In their eponymous anthem, they sang a refrain: "We are a Yellow Pearl . . . and we are half the world." Through my childhood's World's Fair–informed Americana frame, I couldn't help but feeling, "Yes, we are, but why do we seem to always be the *other* half of the world from where we now stand in twentieth-century NYC/USA—the half that is not being considered or even heard?" That same sense of alienation seized every fiber of my being during that 1989 Pro-Democracy movement solidarity march. This feeling only intensified during the following months as sociopolitico support for and media coverage of China's Pro-Democracy movement and the contemporary Chinese voice and disposition faded. For the first time, I felt the full emptiness of the news cycle and outpouring of public empathy and support moving on to the next shiny news object. That autumn, it was the falling of the Berlin Wall, among other historical events. Even the *Village Voice*'s giving a big shout-out to our *Big Character Poster* film by calling it a "Chinese Spinal Tap" could not fill this void . . . or stop the rain.

On that cold and windy afternoon in June 1989, as I stood in the pouring rain outside the Chinese Consulate clutching my umbrella with one hand and raising my fist with the other, I had no idea how to stop the rain . . . but I knew I could never stop searching and working toward that goal.

Two years removed from the Tiananmen Square protests and three years removed from having my creative life forever changed by a reading from *M. Butterfly* by playwright David Henry Hwang himself, Hwang's activism in leading the 1991

Miss Saigon protests strongly, if indirectly, influenced my professional trajectory.

When the musical *Miss Saigon* transferred to Broadway from London's West End in 1991, the producers emphatically, and infamously, announced that, in their estimation, no Asian American actors were capable of performing the lead role of "The Engineer," a Eurasian character. Thus, as producers, they had no choice but to also import the star of the London production, the completely non-Asian actor Jonathan Pryce. It was also announced that for the Broadway production in *our* city, Pryce would continue to perform the role wearing eye prosthetics and skin bronzer to make him appear "more Asian." This was unacceptable on so many levels—especially during the "Gorgeous Mosaic" era of multiculturalism. Many of us took to the streets to protest.

As David Henry Hwang and B. D. Wong were the only established Asian American Broadway artists at that time, they bravely led a very high-profile resistance against this "yellow face" casting of a non-Asian actor in a Eurasian role in one of those rarest of craft- and career-building opportunities for an Asian American actor, or for any actor: a leading role on Broadway. Not to mention, they were also orchestrating the pushback on the public marginalization of an entire artistic community. This campaign soon had the backing of American Actors' Equity—whose members were weighing in more on the side of nationalistic employment sovereignty than on the side of ethnic artistic liberation.

Looking back, I can see that this conflict was very complex. As an artist, you never want to give a legal or governing entity the right to dictate artistic choices. I just wish the *Miss Saigon* producers had been more transparent in their aims in saying that they wanted to keep working with Pryce and not belittle an entire community. But that's where the rubber hits the road in the "perennial culture vs. commerce" wars. As our resistance mounted, the producers threatened to cancel the production, and American Actors' Equity relented. Less than a year later, Jonathan Pryce was on national television hoisting high a Tony Award statuette for his performance as The Engineer on Broadway.

While the collateral cultural shrapnel and skid-mark scars from getting repeatedly run over by the commerce juggernaut may fade some, the wounds never completely heal. Still, Hwang and Wong ignited a brave charge that energized a new generation of artists to become political activists, or, in twenty-first-century parlance, "woke," and ready to continue the fight. From this woke state, what resonates just as strongly as the Asian American artists and activists' unified show of resistance is a postmortem panel discussion during which Jessica Hagedorn bravely pointed out, "How come no one ever says, 'We're fighting so people can have the right to star in this piece of shit'?" And to think, a mere four years prior to the *Miss Saigon* uprising, not one protest sign or dissenting voice was raised in reaction to the primarily Caucasian cast of *Nixon in China* at the Brooklyn Academy of Music.

Following the *Miss Saigon* protests, Wayman Wong, a fellow playwright and Asian American Journalists Association member, referred me to NYU's Graduate Musical Theatre Writing Program. Wong was also the *Daily News* reporter who broke the story of the *Miss Saigon* casting controversy that ignited this resistance. To its credit, this NYU program was heeding the call of the protests and actively sought out Asian American playwrights, lyricists, and composers. Through this outreach NYU had contacted Wayman, who could not pursue this opportunity but recommended me, among others. As I prepared for my NYU interview, it occurred to me that if theatre was alien to me as a child, Broadway musicals were another galaxy . . . on the surface. Scratching a little deeper, through my love of rock 'n' roll song cycles and concept albums, musical theatre—if not Broadway musicals, per se—was in my blood, starting with my very first concert at the legendary Madison Square Garden.

During my second month of junior high school, Rick Wakeman, the flamboyant white cape–wearing keyboard virtuoso for the British "classical progressive rock" bands Yes and Strawbs, brought his art song cycle adaptation of Jules Verne's novel *Journey to the Centre of the Earth* to the Garden. Wakeman was accompanied by his rock band, the National Philharmonic Orchestra and Choir of America, British actor David Hemming as narrator, and a cast of assorted giant dirigible dinosaurs. As an adolescent I had undertaken Wakeman's musical theatre excavation many times by spinning my vinyl record "concept album"—recorded live at London's Royal Festival Hall with all of the previously mentioned players alongside the London Symphony Orchestra and Choir. The MSG concert left a strong impression on my impressionable twelve-year-old mind. Before Wakeman & Co's *Journey to the Centre of the Earth*, my musical theatre appreciation primarily comprised my taking the "Amazing Journey" of The Who's rock opera *Tommy* as a child in the back room of our family's laundry. My brother Herman and I placed *Tommy* on a pedestal from which we sought all varieties of childhood musical, emotional, and spiritual sustenance. All of these formative influences weighed in my decision to apply for this Master of Fine Arts degree program in Musical Theatre Writing.

Along with my acceptance into NYU's GMTWP, I was offered a Yip Harburg Fellowship. Yip is the lyricist extraordinaire of *The Wizard of Oz*, *Finian's Rainbow*, and the timeless Depression-era "is that all there is" anthem "Brother, Can You Spare a Dime?" It was an honor to be a Yip Fellow, and exciting to participate in this pioneering program in its infancy. Back then, class sizes were smaller, and the program was still being led by its founder, Deena Rosenberg—Yip Harburg's daughter-in-law, who was also a proud, card-carrying member of the NYC-DSA (Democratic Socialists of America). The only full-time faculty members were lyricist/librettist Sarah Schlesinger and composer Steve Weinstock.

Then came the exciting and unnerving task of a first creative assignment in a new class. This was just a few years beyond starting my journey as a playwright at The Writer's Voice Creative Writing Program of the 63rd Street YMCA. But those classes lasted only twelve weeks. As the NYU program was for two years, not to mention the vehicle for my working toward an M.F.A., I knew the stakes were higher, so I tried to dig deeper. The result was this monologue:

F.O.B. (Fat Oriental Boy)

I'm not ashamed. I admit it. I used to be an F.O.B. No, I was never one of those Fresh Off the Boat Chinese guys you see all the time in Flushing now. Oh no, I was a "Fat Oriental Boy." Oh yeah, and it was "oriental" not "Asian" during the pre–politically correct days of 1972. And being a fat oriental boy of Chinese persuasion what do you think they called me in P.S. 214? . . . a chunk. And being a chunk off the old block outside of Chinatown in pre-multi-culti NYC, I may as well have needed a green card to enter society. 'Cause let's face it; if just enough flesh is a love handle, then is too much flesh a hate handle? Let me take you back to those halcyon low-stepping days. And those were the good old days, to be young, yellow, fat and free in New York City.

Once upon a time in a tiny bedroom kingdom called Flushing, there lived an F.O.B. laundryman's son. Yes, he came from a long line of stereotypes: his parents ran the only Chinese hand laundry in their neighborhood, and in fact, they were one of the only Asian families in Flushing at the time. So, it was 1972, and he spent his third grade days nestled neatly in his dreams of wanting to be as heroic as Willis Reed of the N.Y. Knicks and to kiss Jennifer, the cute blonde girl who sat in front of him in Assembly. Well, those seemingly temporal goals would have some extraordinary obstacles as all attempts to talk to Jennifer resulted in barely disguised giggling amongst her girlfriends. Now had all the episodes ended that way, nothing out of the ordinary may have happened.

As more of these episodes unraveled, it became clear that the key word in the giggling of Jennifer and her friends was "chink," often alternating with "fat chink." Well, things finally reached a point where he simply did not want to hear it anymore.

One morning in the auditorium during Assembly, intending only to silence the laughter, or have that key word changed, the F.O.B. pushed Jennifer's head—which hit the sharp corner of a hard wood auditorium seat. To everyone's surprise, she turned around with blood seeping out of her forehead like cranberry sauce . . . But it was no Thanksgiving. The F.O.B. just got hysterical and ran out of the auditorium.

Later that hour, he sat crying uncontrollably in front of Jennifer's mother—in the principal's office.

"What happened?" Jennifer's mother finally asked.

But the F.O.B. was still so upset that he couldn't even speak. So he wrote something down on a piece of paper and handed it to Jennifer's mother.

"Jennifer and her friends wouldn't stop calling me . . . a chink," she read aloud.

Jennifer's mother took a deep breath . . . then softly said, "I'm sorry that my daughter was calling you that. She was wrong."

That was the first time that a grown-up ever told that little F.O.B. that he was right. And for the first time, that F.O.B. felt just a little L-U-V in N.Y.C. outside of his parent's laundry.

A true fable of how one chunk flew over the cuckoo's nest.

A child's longing to belong gets challenged daily in that most merciless of arenas, one's grade school. "F.O.B." is a true story—albeit with changed names. So deeply disturbing was this incident that I never discussed this with anyone—not even my brother and childhood confidant, Herman. It took a first creative writing prompt as a graduate student some twenty years after the incident to finally process this traumatic event. In the end, the mother convinced the principal that it wouldn't be necessary to call my parents. I am forever grateful for this parent's progressive foresight to recognize a child on the verge of completely shutting down. Although "Jennifer" and I would go to school together for the next five years—passing each other almost daily in the hallways of P.S. 214 and Junior High School 185 from the ages of ten to fourteen—we never even made eye contact again. I performed "F.O.B." in solo shows and guest reading slots at The Nuyorican Poets Café and elsewhere for years to come. I never once had to fake the fear or the hurt.

▌▌▌

As our entire focus for those two NYU years was on theatre, music, lyric writing and playwriting, and their place in and relationship to the world in different regions and eras, it's no wonder that the GMTWP turned out to be the first and only time school synced-up with all aspects of my life. It greatly helped that my classmates were of all different ages, as well as from varied social, cultural, and artistic backgrounds. All of these factors contributed to school's finally becoming a journey of learning and not just an endless series of academic and social tests.

Our craft workshops were augmented with many guest speakers from "the industry." Cosmos-appropriate, one of the program's first industry guest speakers was the renowned musician and arts entrepreneur Herb Alpert. Rick Wakeman's *Journey to the Centre of the Earth* was released by A&M records, of which Mr. Alpert was the A. In our brief post-presentation conversation, it was clear that only one of us had a fond memory of *Journey*. I strongly suspected that only one of us remembered it at all.

As we learned the original social and artistic context of musical theatre works such as *Showboat, The Three Penny Opera, Oklahoma!, Cabaret, Street Scene, Sweeney Todd,* and *Porgy and Bess,* I came away with a greater appreciation of these works. This was a complete about-face from the way in which most of my generation learned of these musicals. Back then, it was as if these "Broadway classics" were deities of the arts bound up in the plastic wrapping that covered too many living room furniture settings in the suburban and outer borough living rooms of my youth. In that plastic wrapping, nothing can breathe or be felt. The force-feeding of these musicals, as

well as unconvincing Shakespeare-for-grade-school productions, on unsuspecting youths was the cultural equivalent of
enforced castor oil or similar extreme medicines. In most Asian
homes, these cure-alls usually came in the form of wicked-
tasting broths born from days of simmering. We hated these
broths as kids . . . now as adults, we wish we knew how to brew
them.

The students of the NYU program also took turns organizing
musical theatre–appreciation outings. When it was my turn, I
organized a trip down to the Chinatown History Project (now
the Museum of Chinese in America) to show—hell, force—my
classmates and professors to appreciate Cantonese opera. Yes,
what makes us squeamish and even ashamed as children often
becomes a point of pride for us as adults.

Even during this "trip the light: gorgeous mosaic" era in New
York City, I was intrinsically pulled inward to try to respond
to the call of history and legacy and not just compete for instant
contemporary hipster notoriety, although I had certainly
done plenty of the latter while a regular habitué of and some-
time Poetry Slam host and competitor at The Nuyorican Poets
Café. During my NYU days in the early '90s, most of my nights
were spent at the Café. There, I also developed and presented
my punk rap musical, *The Goong Hay Kid*. But even while
this work was being developed and presented in one of the

institutions that defined downtown culture, the fast-talking hipster rhymes and rants of the Chinatown hip-hop "punk-rapper" title character were balanced by slow, introspective Old World scenes with his uncle. My NYU M.F.A. thesis project, *The Last Hand Laundry in Chinatown*, took this historical legacy exploration even deeper. The first study for this musical, "'Twas The Night Before Chinese New Year," was honed orally during readings and slams at The Nuyorican and would also be published in their anthology, *Aloud*.

"'Twas the Night Before Chinese New Year"

'Twas the night before Chinese New Year
And all throughout Chinatown the word was out:
The old man was being hunted down
Like the other from another planet.
His believers at the Pagan Pagoda knew he was gone
But they hung out all night anyway; with hopes that he
*   would return.*
'Twas the night before Chinese New Year
And a dirty kind of quiet ripped up East Broadway in
*   search of a storm,*
but found only the old sewing woman taking the moon out
*   for its nightly walk.*
The birdman of the Bowery left his cages wide open, but
*   the birds would not fly*
For they knew the tedium of surviving on the inside
was much easier than trying to get their wings,
out there in the sweet and sour sky.
But how would the old man survive?
'Twas the night before Chinese New Year
And the red noise of the New Year had not yet begun,
but in a sense had already ended.
Nobody could fall asleep but no one could wake up

as visions of the old man danced in and out of the broken
   neon shadows,
hovering over everybody's bed.
'Twas the night before Chinese New Year
and all throughout Chinatown all the traffic lights stayed
   yellow.
But all the people saw red.

Looking back, "'Twas . . ." was also how I was subconsciously imagining what *Our Town* looked like, felt like, smelled like. As a child I was always searching for an American frame through which to view and process my Old World immigrant Chinese family. Now, as an adult, I was starting to re-create that frame to reflect and include our stories. For *The Last Hand Laundry in Chinatown,* the old man from the poem morphed into a *memento mori* of my parents' lifelong laundry proprietors' struggle as outsiders in a country that never fully accepted them. Through my research, the musical also became an homage to that institutional outsider uphill battle that was The Chinese Hand Laundry Alliance.

A vastly reworked version of *The Last Hand Laundry in Chinatown (A Requiem for American Independents),* with songs by John Dunbar and me, was presented at the legendary La MaMa in the East Village—several years after NYU. This production featured cast members from both *M. Butterfly* and *Miss Saigon*—including Lori Tan Chinn, who portrayed *M. Butterfly*'s scene-stealing Red Guard and in the twenty-first century is winning over TV audiences as the grandmother on *Awkwafina Is Nora from Queens.* In many ways, this production brought this odyssey full circle . . . from The Chinese Hand Laundry Alliance to street protests of *Miss Saigon*, to a Master of Fine Arts degree from NYU. At the 1993 NYU graduation ceremony, none other than Tony Kushner handed me my diploma!

The reworked *Last Hand Laundry in Chinatown (A Requiem for American Independents)* was also published in *Tokens? The NYC Asian American Experience on Stage*, an oral history and play anthology I wrote and edited. For the musical's introduction, I wrote:

"You used to have to buy-in, to be an American.
Now you have to sell-out, to really get some clout."
Sung by Crazy Tom from the title song.

Just as "What are we fighting for?" was the battle cry for social change and awareness in the 1960s and '70s, in the downsizing '90s, that cry became, "What are we working for?" Under the dark shadow of the corporate cleansing of America (cum the world), where the eventual outcome seems to be only one big (brother of a) controlling corporation, almost every working person finds it difficult to build up any personal or professional equity and security. In fact, most find themselves getting ousted from the very institutions to which they have dedicated themselves and built-up.

It is in this ghostly landscape, in which America knows what it is not, but is not exactly sure of—or afraid to admit—what it has become, in which *The Last Hand Laundry in Chinatown (A Requiem for American Independents)* is set. Utilizing contemporary "vaudevillian rock & roll" songs within a traditional musical narrative structure, the piece focuses on the spiritual, financial and ethical effects of gentrification on a second generation Chinese American family in New York City's Chinatown—where

ancient, supernatural Chinese spirits have a head-on colli-
sion with modern, gritty urban realities. Within this frame-
work, the musical also explores the legacy of the pioneering
hand laundrymen and women of Chinese America—of
which my parents were two."

Tokens? celebrates and explores the often-overlooked 1990s
NYC Asian American theatre scene. Asian American identity
and essence were changing. This change was represented on
stage with plays and performance pieces evolving away from
the first wave of primarily plot-driven narratives of identity
politics from the generation of Frank Chin—the first Asian
American playwright to have a play produced Off-Broadway
in New York City. The '90s saw more global, multi-genre works.
The anthology's scripts range from *Sakina's Restaurant*, the
satirical solo performance work on immigration from future
Daily Show correspondent Aasif Mandvi; the irreverent devised theatre work *Big Dicks, Asian Men* from SLANT; and
performance texts from the Peeling the Banana ensemble to
the deeply reverent *SlutForArt* by Muna Tseng and Ping Chong.
SlutForArt is a dance, multimedia, and oral history requiem
for the AIDS devastation of the downtown arts world through
the personal lens of Tseng's brother, photographer/performance
artist Tseng Kwong Chi—a close friend of Keith Haring and
a visual historian of that era. Both Tseng Kwong Chi and Keith
Haring lost their lives to AIDS. Short works from Jessica
Hagedorn, David Henry Hwang, Chiori Miyagawa, Han Ong,
and Ralph Peña round out the stage texts. The Oral History
section of the book, titled "The Verbal Mural," pulls from
interviews with these artists along with Asian American theatre
pioneers Frank Chin; Tisa Chang, founding Artistic Director
of the Pan Asian Repertory Theatre; and the first producers
of Asian American theatre works in New York City, La MaMa's
Ellen Stewart and Wynn Handman of the American Place

Theatre, which first produced Frank Chin. Introductions were written by Chay Yew and Ben Fong-Torres.

Further witness to how Asian American arts and activism were gaining a wider appreciation in 1990s NYC was when *The Goong Hay Kid* became the first play—or full-length performance work—written by an Asian American to be presented at the historic Nuyorican Poets Café. This was also my first full-fledged production—not just a one- or even three-night stand. Following a workshop at the Multicultural Playwrights Festival of the now-defunct Seattle Group Theatre—where I was honored to work with the late, great Native American playwright William S. Yellow Robe Jr. as my first dramaturg—the play was ready for New York City.

The Nuyorican Poets Café is the storied center of spoken word and activism founded in the 1970s by a group of New York City Puerto Rican artists/activists led by Miguel Algarín and Miguel Piñero. In the early 1970s, Piñero became the first Puerto Rican playwright to be produced on Broadway with *Short Eyes*. This was almost a decade before Lin-Manuel Miranda was even born. It was an enormous affirmation for me and many of my fellow Asian American spoken-word, theatre, and music artists that Miguel Algarín, as well as the Café's theatre and Poetry Slam directors, Rome Neal and Bob Holman, welcomed us to that singular community that is The Nuyorican Poets Café.

In the early 1990s, the Nuyorican Poets Café was a magical place. Set after set, night after night, a succession of brilliant poets, spoken-word, dance, musical, and theatre performance artists graced the Café stage. The brilliance onstage was often matched with equally creative heckling/encouragement from the rowdy yet erudite audience members. And you never knew who would pop up unannounced as a special guest on the bandstand, open mic, or dance floor. One night, after an amazing set of Latin jazz, the stagehands put down a square of special flooring and then pointed a number of microphones at that floor. A few minutes later, Savion Glover was workshopping what would later become his Tony Award–winning tap dance choreography for the Off-Broadway and Broadway game changer *Bring in 'da Noise, Bring in 'da Funk*.

I also became the host of the Wednesday Night Slam Open as well as one of Bob Holman's backup hosts for the Friday Night Open Slam for a few years. In late-twentieth-century late-night television parlance, I often called myself the Joe Garagiola to Bob's Johnny Carson. Standing on the stage for a Slam night or any night, you could feel the power and energy in that room. I found myself in the center of a community of artistry with a singular level of primal talent and diversity that I had not witnessed before or since. The Café felt like the heart and soul of New York City's "Gorgeous Mosaic."

For the Nuyorican Poets Café production of *The Goong Hay Kid*, I also had the added bonus of being the rhythm guitarist in the production's "punk-rap" pit band! Playing the title role was Ken Leung—now also a renowned film and television actor. Before each performance, director Rome Neal would gather the entire cast, band, and crew into a circle on one of the upper floors of the Café to share what we were grateful for or troubled by that night. The circle check-in concluded with a *griot*-styled call-and-response chant of the chorus from the Rare Earth song "I Just Want to Celebrate." On opening night, I became very emotional during the circle check-in. I started crying as I lamented the fact that my Dad would not physically be in attendance for this or any of my premieres. The tears continued to flow as I shared how grateful I was for everyone in the circle and all of the spirits and humans downstairs in the Café—especially The Empress Mother and Herman, who were in the house that night. For this production, we used an audio recording of The Empress Mother singing "People's Lives Are Like Dreams."

During the pre-show "curtain speech," Rome and Miguel graciously introduced The Empress Mother, and she took a flashy bow for the ages—I had to get the show-biz gene from somewhere! Every night, the prologue and epilogue ended with a recording of The Empress Mother singing "People's Lives Are Like Dreams." On opening night, the voice of the play's prologue and epilogue as well as the embodiment of its conscience and soul was seated at one of the Café's front tables.

Throughout the show, I kept watching The Empress Mother and Herman. I smiled as Herman visually reacted to the show's laughs and cries and everything in between. I was even more moved by The Empress Mother's static facial expression. While she was clearly proud to be there, and I couldn't have been prouder to have her there, it was a heartbreaking visual and visceral revelation of the language barrier between us all these years. As mother and youngest son we shared so much. Yet as a writer, I could never fully share with her what was most important and vital to me. I regretted even more that I could not fluently speak, let alone write, any dialect of Chinese.

In the end, The Gorgeous Mosaic was a most healing, empowering, and exhilarating period. It made most of us accept and process a more nuanced and complex portrait of who we were as a city, a society, and a world. Yet, inevitably, every answer of affirmation that The Gorgeous Mosaic offered posed even more complicated questions. The underside of the "Gorgeous

Mosaic" era was the fight and resiliency required to celebrate and represent our unique identities, communities, and cultures. Scenes and worlds often change on a whim. Other times it takes an epidemic and everything in between. Each and every performance and work of art is a statement and celebration of being. All representation is personal and political. We must seize the moment and realize it while we can.

Chapter 11

:::

Commencement Ceremonies: Leaving Flushing

ALTHOUGH MY BROTHER Herman had not lived in The Second Flushing Palace of The Eng Dynasty for many years, he lived nearby on Long Island and would regularly stop by for visits as well as to be our invaluable, all-purpose Mr. Fix-it for the property. In the spring of 1993, a month before my NYU graduation, Herman announced that he was moving to L.A. to continue his career as a musician, sound engineer, and technician. In the twenty-first century, he would go on to become a guitar technician for the likes of Bob Dylan and fellow Queens native Paul Simon, among others. In a most timely coincidence of pop culture and graduate school karma, the double-album rock opera that was *the* childhood compass in so many ways for Herman and me arrived as a Broadway musical—rebranded as *The Who's Tommy* . . . just as I was completing my M.F.A. degree in musical theatre writing!

To prepare for his move to L.A., Herman was selling most of his musical gear, including his beloved and sturdy British-manufactured Hiwatt amps that he had originally sought and bought in emulation of Pete Townshend. The guitarists in the *Tommy* Broadway pit band saw Herman's ad and purchased all of his Hiwatt amps in an effort to further replicate the sound of The Who on Broadway.

As one of many NYU program perks, we students received free tickets to see *The Who's Tommy*. Seeing this musical would be one of the last nights out for Herman and me before his move to L.A. In addition to *Tommy's* being an emotional road map for our bonding childhood years, the rock opera's songs were the first ones Herman had learned to play. The then–newly adapted Broadway musical began with the overture's thunderous opening guitar chords being played as the house lights swiftly went to black. The power chords practically shook the foundation of the storied St. James Theatre. Herman and I smiled at each other with pride, knowing that some of that powerful sound was coming through his old Hiwatt amps. As the overture unfurled, it became clear that *Tommy's* raw musical power was still as palpable as when I first heard the rock opera as a child in our laundry's back room. Back then, *Tommy* was a security blanket and buffer between childhood innocence and our parents' viciously confrontational arranged marriage. Now I was an adult sitting in the darkened audience of a Broadway theater a quarter-century later, and the concept album and now musical became a primal portal to process unfinished business with the past and the dead.

In the scene and song following the overture, Tommy's parents lecture him, "You didn't hear it, you didn't see it," about their crimes and infidelities that were symbolic of Britain's broken promises to its post–World War II generation. I flashed back to a vivid childhood scene I had been blocking out, one that I remembered but never fully comprehended or processed . . . until seeing *The Who's Tommy* on Broadway . . . with Herman just as he was about to leave the NYC area for L.A.

While I was hiding away listening to *Tommy* in our laundry's back room, in the middle and front rooms The Empress Mother's accusations of my Dad's infidelities started rising to loud rants and even louder actions—often resulting in two- three-day disappearing acts from each parent.

The green and pink neon sign bearing "Foo J. Chin Hand Laundry," Dad's paper name and my parents' professional trade, was always the centerpiece of the display windows of every laundry my family owned and operated. Soon, the neon sign in the laundry window started getting company. Just under the neon sign, across the bottom front expanse of the store's display window (which was actually about thigh-high, designed to accommodate sightlines for retail displays), The Empress Mother hired a painter to create a three-foot-high banner with white capital letters that spelled out "LAUNDRY," against a good luck Chinese red background with white trim. An "address banner" was painted on the side panel in the same color scheme. Soon, even that was not enough. The Empress Mother started taping pictures of Chinese landscapes above the banner and beside the neon sign like amulets. Now our laundry's entire front window, side panel, and entrance were all covered to assure that Dad's allegedly wandering eyes would be without sightlines. Then, the only natural light that shone through the windows was between the dusty glass tubes of our laundry's neon shingle. No wonder the "deaf, dumb, and blind"–informed artwork of the original *Tommy* double LP foldout resonated so strongly during repeated plays in the back room. Did I hear it? Did I see it?

Unfortunately, by the ending of the show, it was clear that the Broadway musical version of *Tommy* had been significantly sanitized for a family-friendly audience. Still, it was thrilling to experience the music that had forever changed Herman and me come alive again on stage after all those years. The fact that the power chords that served as the Broadway orchestra's baton for that finale and the entire musical were blasting through Herman's old Hiwatt amps eight days—or rather eight shows—a week was a most fitting coda to our childhood together, and now the end of this chapter of Herman's Flushing and East Coast life. Now, just as there will always be a little piece of *Tommy* in the hearts of Herman and me, there were also little pieces of Herman's equipment in the Broadway production. Well, a few not so little pieces . . . and awfully loud ones at that.

Following Herman's move to L.A., The Second Flushing Palace was now just The Empress Mother and me. Although I had long seen her slowing down throughout the late 1990s, I was still in denial about her ultimate passing. During the final decade of The Empress Mother's life, I did the shopping. I did the cooking. I changed her diapers, all while managing and driving her to all of her doctor appointments. One night as I tucked her in, she just looked up and said, *"Koy hoe doy. Nee oh-nye loy?"* ["Such a good son, where did you come from?"]. I touched her stomach and replied, "Here." She smiled.

Caring for The Empress Mother became my purpose. Perhaps this purpose was rooted in a sense of duty to Old World filial obligations. Perhaps this purpose was an escape from all of the New World pressures and disappointments that existed just outside The Second Flushing Palace of The Eng Dynasty. Perhaps out of a combination of both, things actually made sense for a little while.

The one and only time I said aloud, "I can accept that my mother is going to pass away" was on the night of November 8,

2002. I shared this with my girlfriend, who is now my wife, Wendy Wasdahl, as well as with the heavens and the cosmos. Within twelve hours, by 12 noon on November 9, 2002, The Empress Mother had left this mortal world. Many times, the heavens ally with mortals to make a final peace with their immediate loved ones before their final earthly passage.

The Tibetan Book of the Dead teaches us that the last sense to expire is hearing. Before the paramedics arrived to remove The Empress Mother's now-inanimate body, I got down on both knees and whispered my final pledges of love and gratitude. I hope she heard me. I know she felt me.

The week and aftermath of the family's convening to plan and carry out The Empress Mother's funeral was one of the most difficult times of my life. Just as raw and primally painful as The Empress Mother's passing were the unspoken but loudly acted out acknowledgments that her passing was also the end of our family, "The Eng Dynasty," as we knew it. For some members, this reckoning only deepened our silent, difficult-to-articulate grief. For others it also marked a time for last licks to avenge decades-simmering rifts. Although we had already grown quite distant from one another—literally and figuratively, each one of us knew: all bets were off in terms of future family obligations and even structure. Sometimes, the death and passing of a loved one can bring people and a family together as had happened with the passing of my Dad a quarter-century prior. The Empress Mother's passing had quite the opposite impact.

For The Empress Mother's memorial service at her beloved True Light Lutheran Church in Manhattan's Chinatown, it was decided that her oldest and youngest children would offer eulogies. After my brother Gene spoke, as he had so many times before as a "guest preacher" from the True Light pulpit, I read a verse from "Days," a lyric written by Ray Davies for a song recorded by The Kinks.

"Thank you for the days,
Those endless days, those sacred days you gave me
I'm thinking of the days,
I won't forget a single day believe me
Although you're gone,
You're with me every single day, believe me."

Several months after The Empress Mother's passing, The Eng Dynasty sold its final common holding, The Second Flushing Palace. I moved across the water to an apartment in Jersey City, New Jersey. A few weeks into my Jersey City life, my public farewell to Flushing came via a reading at its gorgeously refurbished Main Street Library. The event was part of a program to celebrate the Museum of Chinese in the America's "Flushing, Queens" exhibit, as well as the PBS/WNET series *Becoming American*. I gave a reading from my first memoir monologue play, *The Flushing Cycle*.

It was truly a homecoming. The room was SRO replete with my Flushing High School English teacher, Madeline Staffanell, and her daughter, my FHS classmate Laura, and, of course, my best friend, Ray Wong, all in attendance.

In a spacious conference room with a floor-to-ceiling window that offered a "greatest hits" panoramic view of downtown Flushing with Shea Stadium, the Unisphere, the World's Fair grounds, and the #7 train tracks in the distance, I gave my reading to a completely simpatico hometown audience of new and old Flushingites. To close the reading, I read a new passage:

Although I no longer live in Flushing,
Flushing will always be my emotional abode.
No Exit is final.
Every exit is just a passageway on to another road.

At verse's end, the electric curtain next to the panoramic window suddenly started shaking in place. I spilled my cup of water. It felt like the entire building shook for a few seconds.

Chapter 12

***

Village Pilgrimage
for a Marriage Blessing

MANY HAVE OFTEN described the condition of losing a second parent as akin to being orphaned. The passing of a second parent, "The Empress Mother," left me feeling unmoored, adrift between the mortal and the eternal life. For the forty years that we were on the same plane and planet, my worldview was entirely tethered to my station in this family as the youngest child, brother, and, later, caretaker of The Empress Mother within our Old World, illegal immigrant Chinese family structure and dynamic. Facing the future was something I was incapable or unwilling to do as this necessitated accepting a world in which The Empress Mother, along with my identity and purpose, would no longer exist. Scars from often-violent memories of my parents' arranged marriage also obscured future projections of what a marriage of my own would be like and feel like.

After The Empress Mother's passing and the selling of The Second Flushing Palace—the only home I had known for almost a quarter-century—the option of "leaving home" was off the table. Home had left me. As I moved from Flushing to Jersey City, it was under the paralyzing cloud of owning up to the fact that I was first processing things at the age of forty that most people process at the age of twenty.

Eight months after The Empress Mother's passing, I started living with Wendy Wasdahl—first in my apartment in Jersey City and then in hers in Lower Manhattan. Meeting and falling in love with her, I had finally found heart and soul sanctuary that I could feel and touch. I was no longer relying on pop culture preferences or even artistic choices to placate the longing to belong. This longing to belong was now resolved by life choices . . . as well as by resolving the choices that life makes for us.

We met at a dinner party on New Year's Eve 1998–99 in Park Slope, Brooklyn. The dinner was at the home of my friends Anne Shonbrun and Alan Siege and co-hosted by a newly en-gaged couple comprising one of Wendy's closest friends, Amy Schwartzman, and Peter Brightbill—whom I met on the first day of my first playwriting class at The Writer's Voice a decade prior. My first conversation with Wendy took place seated be-tween one long-time married couple and another couple that was soon to be married. Within minutes we found we shared similar yet vastly different experiences in what used to be called "downtown theatre." Whereas I always seem to find or at least define myself as being on the fringes of . . . *everything*, Wendy developed artistically in a unique and supportive community as the founding artistic/producing director and principal per-former of The Shared Forms Theatre company. Shared Forms was a pioneering force in the then-burgeoning SoHo/Tribeca arts scene—and a frequent resident theatre company with The Wooster Group. As we conversed further, I could feel Wendy's passion, knowledge, and wicked sense of humor enveloped within her indefatigable and uncompromising commitment to New York City, the arts, and the world. Yet it was a decidedly uptown theatre conversation through which we first bonded.

"I've actually been seeing a lot of Broadway lately," shared Wendy.

"I've only seen Paul Simon's *The Capeman* . . . but I saw it twice," I related.

"So did I!"

"Amazing! Not many people have even seen it once."

"It was interesting to see so many techniques that we all developed off-off-off now being incorporated on Broadway," reflected Wendy. "It's a shame how it got slammed in the press."

"And who are they to tell Paul Simon how to tell a story with music," I strongly defended my fellow Queens native.

"It's almost midnight, let's get ready," summoned our hostess, Anne.

After listening to Prince's "1999" to commemorate the moment, the group walked up "the slope" to Prospect Park for New Year's Eve fireworks. Wendy's having a bum knee that night allowed us to linger behind and continue our conversation—just the two of us.

Years later, I would learn of our vastly different reactions to our respective invitations. From her Tribeca perspective, Wendy was reluctant to go out on New Year's Eve "all the way out to Brooklyn to a dinner party where there were mainly couples . . ." From my Flushing perspective, a New Year's Eve dinner party in Park Slope instantly became my social highlight of the season . . . I would have arrived on the 29th if I could have. All in all, the final year of the twentieth century could not have gotten off to a more promising start.

Wendy moves through this world with a loving grace and glow. Over meals or under pressure, on the streets or on the stage, in rehearsal rooms or classrooms, she has an innate knack for conjuring intimate, illuminating interactions. During her first visits with The Empress Mother, I also started seeing the universal dimensions of Wendy's emotional lingua. By this time, The Empress Mother spent most of her time in bed. Inevitably, she would take Wendy's hand—sometimes laughing but most times weeping—and pour her heart out . . . in Toisan Cantonese . . . a language Wendy, who is of eastern and northern European descent, did not speak but responded as if. After a handful of these bilingual tête-à-têtes, as family arrived from all over the country for her eightieth-birthday celebration, The Empress Mother routinely introduced Wendy as my wife—even admonishing one of my brothers for introducing her as my girlfriend. Sometimes heart, hands, and empathy supersede words and legal matters.

After three years of our sharing a home, it was the passing of Wendy's second parent, her mother, Ann Brown, in 2007 that was a major catalyst in my proposing marriage. Even though we had been a couple since 1999 and living together since 2004, now that we no longer had the foundation of living parents on this Earth, for me, marriage seemed like the organic next step in our *pas de deux*—a dance for which we had very different entrées. For Wendy, the only child of an only child, this would be her second marriage, while I, the youngest of five children, had long ago forecasted bachelorhood as my destiny.

Wendy's mother, Ann, passed away on March 3, 2007, in a hospital close to The Actors Fund Home in Englewood, New Jersey. The historic retirement facility for Equity Actors was Ann's home since 1980 and was also an inspiration for Neil Simon's play and later film *The Sunshine Boys*. Ann had raised Wendy in San Francisco as a single parent after Wendy's father passed away during her early childhood. Just as with The Empress Mother's passing, the heavens allied with mortals to comfort their immediate loved ones on the final earthly passage of a loved one. Wendy got to visit her mother one last time in the hospital when Ann assured her that she would be OK and it was fine for Wendy to go home. By the time she returned to Lower Manhattan from Englewood, Ann had passed this mortal realm . . . at peace that she had comforted her daughter before leaving.

Ann Brown was an actress, activist, and an original cast member of the ILGWU-inspired musical *Pins and Needles*. This little union musical that had a celebrated Broadway run highlighted by a command performance at the White House for President Franklin Delano Roosevelt and his wife, and Ann's heroine, Eleanor Roosevelt, in 1938—the same year that *Our Town* opened on Broadway.

We were able to bring together Ann and The Empress Mother to celebrate two Mother's Days. Once at Ann's favorite restaurant on Route 9W in Englewood Cliffs, and a second at our beloved International House of Pancakes on Northern Boulevard in Flushing. The Moms were the same height and even looked somewhat identical. By this point, both Moms had equal amounts of slumping senior posture and both sported white, short-cropped "senior citizen" hairdos. Although one of them spoke some English and one of them spoke zero Toisan Chinese, they were able to communicate. Wendy and I still smile at the memory of the Chinese Mom sitting next to the Jewish Mom as our new family tableau.

I proposed to Wendy on her birthday, May 5, 2007—two months and two days after her Mom's passing. Although plans were already in place for a trip to Hong Kong, Toisan, and several other cities in China, after Wendy's Mom's passing and our engagement, the Toisan part of the trip became a pilgrimage for a spiritual blessing of our marriage.

Wendy never met my Dad. Still, he has hovered as a huge presence. The decision to search for Dad's Eng village and not The Empress Mother's Chin village, or both, came down to a simple practicality . . . wrapped in all of the complexities of ancestry tracing after both parents had passed away. In this void, we children who cannot read, write, or, for the most part, speak our ancestral language were left grasping at straws. (This was long before ancestry.com and other easily accessible gene-alogy sources.) With all of the complications associated with The Empress Mother's passing, arrangements were never made to obtain the correct Chinese calligraphy of her ancestral village background that was to be carved onto her headstone. Instead, we had the calligraphy of Dad's village that was on his headstone duplicated under The Empress Mother's name and birth and death dates. Thus, in seeking a spiritual blessing for our marriage, Wendy and I set out to find my Dad's Eng village and not The Empress Mother's Chin village of Toisan.

After the reopening of China to Western commerce and travelers in the 1970s, it was a common twentieth-century rite of passage for many Chinese Americans of Toisanese descent to make a pilgrimage to their ancestral village. As the Toisanese dominance in Chinatowns and Chinese communities through-out North America declined in the twenty-first century, so has this rite-of-passage pilgrimage. In 2007, Wendy and I were going for a very different reason, but we still faced the challenges of Toisan's being off the travel and tourism grid—even in the extremely tourist-accommodating twenty-first-century China. Thus, after numerous fruitless queries about traveling to Toisan with conventional travel agents, the next step of this pilgrimage consisted of countless cold weather treks across Worth Street to Chinatown—scouring sundry "informal travel agents" and ultimately winding up at the Eng Family Association.

As one of the connotations of Eng is "5," it's no surprise that the Eng Family Association is located at 5 Mott Street. One cold winter morning, I climbed the well-worn stairs to the Eng Family Association. I opened the door with great anticipation, only to be greeted by the sound of mahjong tiles being shuffled furiously and the sight of tables and tables of elderly men at the top of their game. In my hands were color photos of my parents' headstones. The carved calligraphy of their lifelines were my only visual clues to finding the village. My sole verbal clue was *sly chock I lung*," the one phrase that I faintly remember as being "the name" of their village. Like the mahjong tiles, I started shuffling around the room trying to get someone's attention to show them my photos. The mahjong-playing men didn't even look up from their games.

Finally, a non-mahjong-playing man emerged from another room. I showed him my photos and told him that I was trying to get some information on how to locate my father's village. He shook his head and said . . . nothing. As he started to walk away, I desperately mumbled, *"sly chock I lung . . . ?"* Immediately, he turned around and sprang to life. He looked again at the photos of my parents' headstones and directed me to a bookstore a few blocks away on Mott Street.

"There, you can buy a map of Toisan in Chinese," instructed the Eng Family Association elder—suddenly showing interest, and, dare I say it, concern.

"Bring that map here and I will show you the area where your father's village is. I will also show you where there are hotels where you can hire a driver to help you find the village."

░░░

A few months later, Wendy and I were passengers in a car traversing the rural roads of southern China being driven by a hired driver. The driver was masterfully navigating increasingly bumpy roads when a monsoon-like storm suddenly materialized—turning the blue sky black and unleashing a wicked downpour of biblical proportions. We stopped numerous times as the driver couldn't see out through the windshield. In my shaking hands was the Toisan map purchased on Mott Street, with my father's village circled in red from the accommodating man at the Eng Family Association.

Finally, the sky and the downpour lightened up a little and we were able to proceed during this stretch of more clement weather. The driver dutifully stopped every few villages to ask for directions and help. After several of these consultations and a combination of paved and unpaved pathways, we finally turned onto a dirt road off of a main paved highway. The road was marked with a simple "5" on its sign. I took this sign to be a sign, given that Eng also connotes 5. As we started driving the way of the "5," the monsoon-like deluge returned.

We reached a fork in the road. The driver stopped, turned the engine off, and got out of the car. Somehow, he managed to light a cigarette in the midst of this sudden monsoon. He took a long, slow drag and contemplated his short-term duty versus his long-term well-being. Finally, he got back into the car. He didn't start up the car or even look at us.

"Too dangerous. Can't go today," the driver concluded.

Wendy and I were in an instant manic panic.

"Please, sir," Wendy began pleading. "You don't know how much this means to us."

"Look outside," the driver countered.

"Maybe we can wait a little," I began to beg, trying hard not to weep or have a heart attack . . . or both. "I've been waiting my whole life to see my father's village. . . ."

The driver let out a big sigh, took a few anxious staccato puffs of his cigarette, and revved up the engine.

Later, on the way back to the hotel, we realized that the driver had bravely navigated narrow eddies or aisles that bordered rice paddies that had flooded during the severe rain . . . our car could have easily capsized in one or two of these rows. Finally, after negotiating a few more treacherous muddy country lakes, I mean lanes, we reached *"sly chock I lung"* . . . my father's village.

The torrential downfalls had passed, but it was still drizzling. All of the village residents were still indoors. The sole resident who was outdoors to greet us was a water buffalo. The buffalo was tied to a sort of village gate that welcomed you to this tiny assemblage of assorted farming huts and *hutong* housing comprising that bizarre mixture of equal parts Chinese and Portuguese architecture that was unique to this region of China.

Beyond this seemingly transplanted *hutong* cluster was a beautiful mountain range and what appeared to be endless rows of rice fields as far as my city boy eyes could see. With the sky bathed in a patina of post-thunderstorm haze, it looked like a Chinese scroll painting of a fable or other timeless tale. I was completely overwhelmed. I just handed my camera to Wendy and asked her to take as many photos as possible. I held the umbrella and pretended to act as her guide and interpreter.

We wandered the narrow, empty village alleyways between houses teeming with rain runoff and God knows what else. Soon the rain stopped, and the villagers started emerging. Our outsider presence was immediately sensed. A gentleman who seemed to be the Official Village Elder walked over to our driver and started asking questions. The driver showed him the color photos of my parents' headstones. The Village Elder and some others came over to greet us.

The Village Elder said he knew my father. Being that my father left this village almost eight decades before, I think this was more hospitality than reality. Still, we accepted the welcome . . . and for the first and only time in three trips to China, my limited Toisanese was perfectly understood. I was able to have a conversation in my father and mother's language somewhere outside of our laundry and the Toisan-centric Chinatowns of my childhood. This must be the place.

The ominous storm clouds dominating the Toisan sky brought to mind one of The Empress Mother's rainy-day refrains of how her arthritis was a result of living through wartime conditions during the Japanese occupation of China. I wish The Empress Mother had wanted to visit her Toisan village when she and I first traveled to China in 1987. But she had her reasons that were grounded in painful memories of living through a broken arranged-marriage family, a national civil war, foreign occupation, and the beginnings of a revolution all before she was twelve years old! Then there were the mundane but costly concerns of a village homecoming. The Empress Mother was well aware of the late-twentieth-century custom whereby homecoming "American Toisanese" were expected to bring the gamut of the latest high-end consumer appliances and toys to their village brethren. On that trip, The Empress Mother and I visited Hong Kong, Guangzhou, Guilin, and Beijing, but not Toisan.

After visiting several Toisan village homes, Wendy and I entered one in which the family had several young children. We immediately offered them the toys and candies we'd brought with us. The household's Mom responded with a smiling *"umm soy"*—meaning, "You didn't have to. Really."

As I watched the children play in huts and dirt and on unpaved flooring, I tried to process how that could have been my childhood . . . how this *was* the childhood of my parents, grandparents, and their parents. This was my parents' "Flushing." Their *Our Town.* Wendy and I had completed our pilgrimage to seek a spiritual blessing of our marriage. We would wed on the next New Year's Day—during the auspicious "Year of the Golden Pig" that comes around once every five Chinese Zodiac cycles or every sixty years.

Our wedding was held in a friend's loft a few blocks away from our home in Lower Manhattan. The wedding ceremony band consisted of my brother Herman on guitar and vocals and his then–ten-year-old son, Tyler, on drums. Herman and Tyler musically walked the bride down the aisle to Leonard Cohen's "Dance Me to the End of Love." We walked up the aisle as husband and wife to The Kinks' "Better Things." On that first day of 2008, we completed the first chapter of a journey that began on the final night of 1998.

Chapter 13

Life Dances On:
Our Town in China

"We Are the Champions":
Teaching the Chinese Roots of *Our Town* . . .
in Hong Kong

IT'S THE MORNING after an improbable theatrical triumph at the City University of Hong Kong. We are celebrating the previous night's performance of "Hong Kong Time Capsule 2011"—original plays written and performed by the students in response to Thornton Wilder's *Our Town*. The plays and production were developed in a workshop that Wendy and I created and directed. The students blast "We Are the Champions" through the classroom sound system. They begin a victory dance circle and invite us to join in.

"I've paid my dues . . ." Freddie Mercury begins the sing-along and *dance-a-bration*. We join the circle—hand-in-hand, arms raised in joyous reverie. We are all singing along at the top of our lungs with Queen's timeless international 1970s arena rock anthem. Elevated by the love in the room and the glow on the students' faces, I was also happily surprised that these twenty-first-century college students chose a song from my teenage years—years before the biopic *Bohemian Rhapsody* reintroduced Queen to new generations. When I first heard "We Are the Champions" back in Flushing, I was a little younger than these students and my fingernails were painted black, just like Freddie Mercury's. As we circled round to shout out the first iconic chorus, Wendy and I privately acknowledged two other unlikely stage triumphs: her performing in a new play at Hong Kong's Fringe Club, and my performing my memoir monologue, *The Last Emperor of Flushing*, in our family's ancestral Guangdong Province. Memories of all three recent theatre blessings brought a huge smile to my face and solace to the soul.

As we chanted and danced to Queen with the City U students, I closed my eyes and thought back to my first trip to Hong Kong and China. My late mother, or The Empress Mother as she is anointed in *The Last Emperor of Flushing*, spiritually slipped into the *dance-a-bration* between Wendy and me. We each took one of her hands. Floating on Brian May's power chords, I was transported back twenty-four years to 1987. I was guiding The Empress Mother by the hand through the busy lobby of the New World Hotel, en route to the taxi to the airport for our flight back to the States. As I took my parting glances around the densely populated and ultra-vibrant cityscape, I wondered if I would ever come back to Hong Kong. If I did, whose hand would I be holding? Never in my wildest dreams did I think I would return a married man, a playwright, and, with my wife and the spirit of The Empress Mother, holding the hands of some of Hong Kong's brightest young students. Even further from my mind's eye was that we would be dancing in celebration of a playwriting and performance workshop inspired by the Chinese influence on Thornton Wilder's play *Our Town* . . . and then have, through that workshop, an opportunity to perform a monologue play about my family in Guangzhou in English.

The performance and City U workshop were a result of a Fulbright Specialist residency grant in Theatre/U.S. Studies. The unlikely catalyst for this residency, as well as my writing of *The Last Emperor of Flushing* as a stage play, was *Our Town*, Thornton Wilder's seminal Americana drama. *Our Town* famously features no set and a minimum of props to create an expressionistic and minimalist meditation on mortality and community. Midway through the first scene, you realize that all of the town's characters have already passed away. They are not living mortals. They are timeless spirits. In effect, *Our Town*'s fictitious Grover's Corners, New Hampshire, is not the quintessence of small-town New England quaintness but rather a global village of mind, a sovereign-free state of soul.

I first saw *Our Town* on Broadway, New Year's Eve 1988–89— the final evening of that double 8, double happiness year of discovery and reinvention. This was Lincoln Center Theater's landmark production directed by Gregory Mosher and featuring the late, great monologist Spalding Gray as the Stage Manager. That production also celebrated the half-centennial since *Our Town*'s 1938 Broadway debut. For neophyte theatre practitioners at the time like me, who were just "cutting our teeth" on raw, "downtown" post-punk/street-art-infused theatre, spoken-word literature, and visual art, Spalding Gray's casting was the perfect bridge between "downtown and uptown" experimental and traditional theatrical sensibilities. After all, Gray was also a founding member of The Wooster Group, one of the most influential and inventive experimental theatre groups that nurtured and even guided many of the post-punk, post-modernist practitioners of downtown theatre.

While I was very moved when I first saw the play on Broadway, reengaging with this work after the passing of a second parent was profound. After the passing of The Empress Mother, I moved from Flushing to Jersey City. As I unpacked my tangible baggage there in early 2003, a hard cover copy of *Our Town* somehow seemed to gleam as the key to unlock the mystery of finding the means and meaning to continuity and carrying on. On a break from unpacking I took the play over to the Jersey City Public Library on Van Vorst Park and reread it. In my newly orphaned state of having recently buried the second of two parents, I was convening with the spirits in the mist around us perhaps even more than the mortals in our midst. Though I couldn't qualify or quantify it then, there was an even deeper, subconscious connection to *Our Town*.

Though no one will ever confuse my hometown of Flushing, Queens, with the fictitious Grover's Corners of *Our Town*—or my parents' Chinese hand laundry with any of that town's Mom-and-Pop businesses—those families and my family lived in a world and a home that seemed to belong to another time and place; one that we could feel but never touch. Almost immediately after I finished rereading *Our Town,* I started writing what would become *The Last Emperor of Flushing.*

Our Town is universally acknowledged as forever changing the landscape of the American theatre for being one of the first commercially successful American plays to require no set and only a handful of modernist props. Through this stripped-down presentation, the play challenges, even demands that audiences look deeper into the nuanced drama being performed before them. What is less commonly discussed is that one of the play's primary world theatre influences is Chinese opera. I first became aware of the play's Chinese artistic lineage while preparing to teach a class on *Our Town* in 2006. As part of my class preparation, many friends, colleagues and sources pointed to exploring Wilder's friendship with Gertrude Stein and Alice B. Toklas. I went over to Strand Books, the legendary used bookstore that also serves as a spiritual portal to the storied 4th Avenue bookstall lane of New York City lore, and tracked down *The Letters of Thornton Wilder and Gertrude Stein* by Edward M. Burns, Ulla E. Dydo and William Rice (himself a celebrated downtown theatre artist). Immediately, I loved that Stein sometimes refers to Wilder as "Thorny" as only she can. Then, the following passage caught my attention, when Wilder writes to Stein:

> . . . Guess who may act the long lanky New England Talkative Stage-Manager in it (who as in the Chinese theatre hovers about the action, picking his teeth, handing the actors their properties and commenting drily to the audience)—Sinclair Lewis.

With further research, I learned that Thornton Wilder lived part of his childhood in Hong Kong and Shanghai when his father was U.S. Consul General to those cities in the 1910s. While living there, he was exposed to many different forms of Chinese theatre and culture. In the 1930s, Wilder saw Peking (as it was called then) opera master Mei Lanfang on Broadway just as he was starting to compose *Our Town*. The minimalist staging and performance aesthetic of Peking opera, as well as many of its supernatural ghost-spirit characters, played heavily on Wilder's creation of the play.

Five years after stumbling upon this lesser-discussed Chinese lineage of *Our Town* and twenty-three years after first seeing the play on Broadway, Wendy and I found ourselves leading a devised theatre workshop in which twenty-first-century students from Hong Kong and China would write and perform short plays in response to *Our Town*. Although the residency was grounded in a 1938 play, we worked with the students to dramatize their current lives for an evening of short plays that was to be called "Hong Kong Time Capsule 2011." The title and theme were both inspired by a scene from Act I of *Our Town*, when the townspeople of Grover's Corners are creating a time capsule for the cornerstone of a new bank being built downtown. The good folks of Grover's Corners endowed their time capsule with:

A copy of the *New York Times*
A copy of Mr. Webb's *Sentinel* (Grover's Corners town newspaper)
The Bible
The Constitution of the United States
A copy of William Shakespeare's plays
. . . and quite meta-narratively and meta-physically, the script of *Our Town*

Building on this scene would prove to be a good starting point in helping the students connect their passion through theatre craft. The students were amazed that this Americana play has some Chinese roots and immediately recognized the Chinese opera element of the supernatural narrative being conveyed by spirits of recently deceased beings. Then, the students had another interpretation of *Our Town*.

"Are those families in the play . . . like most of our families?" shyly questioned one male student.

"Not sure what you mean . . ." I responded.

A female student who appeared to be the male student's girlfriend followed up: "I think he means that, you know, many Chinese families started from arranged marriages . . . " then trailed off as all of the other students started smiling.

"Oh, I know," I related. "My parents had an arranged marriage."

Some students seemed surprised.

"Alvin's parents are from Toisan," added Wendy, "from nearby Guangdong Province."

"So are the parents in the play . . . " resumed the first male student to speak out.

". . . are they from arranged marriages?" sensed Wendy.

"Yes," confirmed the female student.

"It doesn't say so in the text," I concluded. "But I can see how you could interpret those couples as being from arranged marriages."

"So how did you two meet?" the female student cut to the chase of their inquiry.

"That's a long story," I started.

"But we didn't have an arranged marriage," affirmed Wendy.

The students burst into laughter, giving us thumbs-up, peace signs, and one of our most beloved visual memories—forming hearts with their hands and an "A" and a "W" with their fingers.

For our first creative exercise, we asked the students to make two lists of objects or concepts for a time capsule—objects or concepts they feel would best represent Hong Kong and them 1,000 years from now, in 3011. The size of our time capsule was limited only by one's imagination. We had no idea what to expect from our City U students, Hong Kong, or each other—this being the first time that husband and wife were also working as educational theatre collaborators. We were thrilled when the students' time capsule answers exceeded our expectations and quelled our anxieties.

For the Hong Kong section of the time capsule, one prevailing theme was a growing concern and distrust that China's central government in Beijing was beginning to backtrack on the "One Country, Two Systems" reunification agreement. This was the agreement brokered between Hong Kong and China in 1997 when HK ceased being a British colony and was returned to the People's Republic of China. In this context, many students chose to preserve the stalls, carts, tools, and utensils used by their beloved curbside and alleyway hawkers of street food and other local goods. They were already sensing a Beijing-directed crackdown on these street vendors—an essential element of Hong Kong's street life DNA. Many other students chose to preserve Victoria Harbour itself—the "fragrant harbor" for which Hong Kong is named. With increasing land reclamation (known as "landfill" in New York) already making the harbor narrower every year, the students feared that it will soon no longer exist. Samples of Hong Kong water and air were also popular time capsule choices. The students wanted to see if the quality of either would improve in 1,000 years.

But this was also still glamorous Hong Kong. Thus, the fashionista contingent of the class chose to include their Louis Vuitton handbags, or "LVs" as they called them, in the time capsule. The stylish students also explained how receiving an LV from a beau was the twenty-first-century equivalent of wearing someone's ring to signify that they were "going steady" in a committed relationship. We took it that LVs also connoted L-U-V in immaterial but mostly material ways.

The LVs notwithstanding, the students' time capsule choices made it clear that while money may well be Hong Kong's *raison d'être* circa 2011, this post–SARS epidemic, post-2007 global economic crisis generation had very different values. Like millennials in America and the world over, the City U students were taking stands to create a greener, more sustainable environment to preserve the city they love in the face of a relentless corporate real estate grab that seems to be the cultural sinkhole of many a major twenty-first-century city.

Looking back, the students' pushback against government overreach in cahoots with corporate corruption were sowing the underground seeds of resistance being planted in Hong Kong and worldwide. Later that fall, those seeds would bloom into the "Occupy Wall Street" movement in the United States. Several years later in Hong Kong, this resistance would come above ground to stay in the 2014 "Umbrella Revolution." Five years later, the Hong Kong resistance became an international focal point of the 2019 "Anti-Extradition Bill/Pro-Democracy" protests. In 2020, tragically, all of the suspicions and concerns expressed by the 2011 Hong Kong students became painfully and tragically true.

█▐█

The next step of the residency was to set about the process of transforming their time capsule objects and concepts, as well as the spirit of Grover's Corners in 1938, into inspiration for a play about Hong Kong during the summer of 2011. Wendy and I worked with the students to construct witty short scenes that dug beneath the shimmering surface of Hong Kong's sophisticated, urbane consumer culture. When it was time to start making that long, laborious journey from the page to stage, we were impressed with how comfortable the City U students were in their bodies as well as in their minds—joyfully jumping through every movement and physical hoop that Wendy posed to them. The resulting initial improvisations and rehearsals, inspired by their time capsule objects and concepts, captured many of the behavioral nuances seen daily on the streets, malls, and MTR trains of their beloved "fragrant harbor." Overall, both the activist and fashionista sides of the class were very enthusiastic, creative, and flat-out funny. They were an absolute joy to be with and made it very easy for Wendy and me to work very well and cohesively as a first-time teaching team. Most of the students had no theatrical experience as practitioners. Perhaps most astonishingly, some had never even seen a play or a musical as an audience member.

This reception Wendy and I received was in stark contrast to that of my first visit to a classroom in China back in Guilin, in 1987. Then, the students were highly suspicious of a Chinese American who could not speak Chinese. In 2011, higher education instruction in Hong Kong and throughout most of China was conducted in English. This new standard greatly helped the City U students welcome this international exchange with a Chinese American professor and a NYC theatre artist, who was also his non-Asian wife, with open arms and minds.

Beyond the classroom, U.S.–Sino relations had also thawed considerably since the chilly relations evident during my first visit to China, in the 1980s. This dynamic also bore almost no resemblance to the post–Cold War reception that my family received in our Chinese hand laundries in New York City of the 1940s to the 1970s. One day, while conferring with a City U staffer who spoke very little English, Wendy wanted to confirm that a piece of theatrical equipment needed to be replaced, not just repaired. To confirm that we were all on the same page, the staffer gave us a thumbs-up and proudly proclaimed, "Yes, change . . . Obama!"

"I've Taken My Bows . . .": Exchanging Artistic Vows, Expanding Marriage Vows

"I've taken my bows . . ." Mr. Mercury starts the second verse of "We Are the Champions" and the second round of the City U *dance-a-bration*. I was elated and elevated by the joy Wendy was sharing with the students. As the lead performer/creator of thirteen original movement theatre works with her company, The Shared Forms Theatre, Wendy is a naturally gifted teacher and director. Though under-utilized in the previous few years, these talents and callings came roaring back to the forefront during our Hong Kong residency. Parallel with getting the City U workshop up and rolling, adjusting to Hong Kong, and our working together for the first time, Wendy was acting in the Hong Kong premiere of a new play, *Bang, Bang* by Rob Mc-Bride, presented by the Not So Loud Theatre Company at the Hong Kong Fringe Club. In preparation I was helping her run lines anywhere we found ourselves with a few spare moments—be it between connecting flights or classes, in crowded airport food courts, or in empty faculty lounges. This rekindling of a primal passion was also a renewal of vows—this time, artistic ones. In celebration of these tandem accomplishments, Wendy's late Mom, Ann Brown, magically joins our *dance-a-bration*. In one hand she takes Wendy's hand, and in the other, The Empress Mother's. As I envision this surreal and magical moment, I have a visceral memory of spreading Ann's ashes into the Hudson River. It was September 8, 2007—what would have been Ann's ninety-fourth birthday. With each palmful of ash, I felt as if I were once again holding Ann's hand and guiding her on one of the many walks Wendy and I used to take her on. As we gazed out from Pier A (for Ann) in Lower Manhattan—with the Holocaust Museum to our right and the Statue of Liberty in the distance to our left, a Spirit Cruise Liner sailed right through the middle of this tableau.

###

Hong Kong has often been called "the Manhattan of Asia." On the streets, Hong Kong feels very much like Manhattan. Both are urbane islands off of their respective mainlands. Both islands are also former British colonies, with Manhattan being liberated in 1776 and Hong Kong in 1997. These dualities and divisions formed the thematic spine of Wendy's Hong Kong production for both of us—on stage and off.

More than one ex-pat has described the Fringe Club as "Hong Kong's La MaMa." Wendy's *Bang, Bang* castmates, crew, and their force-of-nature producer/director, Tom Hope, turn out to be a joy to work with. We wound up spending and enjoying quite a lot of time with them and still keep in touch with some of them. An intensive, condensed rehearsal period was conducted in various venues throughout both islands of Hong Kong—including one in the producer's hippie-throwback beachfront Thai restaurant on Lantau Island! At least on that afternoon, the number of strolling water buffalo families equaled the number of human families taking in the sun and surf.

Bang, Bang explores the conflicted and corrupt origins and media coverage of America's "endless war" in Iraq. The protagonist is a journalist embedded on an American naval vessel. From that vantage point, the play dramatizes that ever-changing state of truth within the struggle for professional dignity and personal liberty that each and every person aboard that vessel is waging with each other as well as within themselves. In numerous ways, Wendy and I were reprocessing these same conundrums throughout our time in Hong Kong as cultural and educational representatives of America via our Fulbright residency grant.

▪▪▪

As with most productions, what went on offstage and after the shows was just as memorable as what happened on the stage. The director/producer was also a member of the legendary Foreign Correspondents' Club—located a few blocks down the hill of Lower Albert Road from the Fringe Club, as well as the houses of government that would soon become synonymous with HK protests in the following years. After every performance, we wound up in the FCC. Often described as the most famous and exclusive press club in the world, the Foreign Correspondents' Club feels and looks like a combination of Rick's Café from *Casablanca* and what one imagined was an upscale Fleet Street pub back in the day when Fleet Street was still the undisputed newspaper and media capital of London. Founded in 1943 in Japanese-occupied Chongqing, the FCC was also based in Shanghai before moving its opulent operations to Hong Kong in 1949 right after the Communist Revolution. After several HK locations, the FCC settled into the prominent building that was a former icehouse in HK's Central district.

As a Chinese American who was happily celebrating with the *Bang, Bang* cast and crew nightly in this living, drinking monument to journalism and colonialism, I had a lot to consider. My grandfather was an opium casualty in New York City's Chinatown, and I have always regarded his fate as a direct result of the Opium Wars. Hong Kong was ceded to Britain as the centerpiece of the Opium Wars defeat settlement. Back in 1997, from my NYC Chinese American perspective, I was happy, even proud to see the end of British rule of Hong Kong as HK was returned to China under the "One Country, Two Systems" agreement. This agreement promised that HK would keep its independent sovereignty while once again becoming part of China. Then, at City University of Hong Kong in 2011, most of our students, as well as protestors I spoke with on the streets, would prefer to return to governance by London instead of by Beijing in a heartbeat. Of course, one wishes there were choices beyond this binary bind. This weighs even more heavily and tragically from the perspective of this writing, as it is becoming official that China will no longer honor its "One Country, Two Systems" agreement.

So as we rightfully celebrate the *Bang, Bang* team in the FCC, like that play's characters we also question whether we are in it but not of it—it being the carefully arranged marriage of journalism and colonialism from different eras and angles but on the same global scale. While I completely reject British colonialism politically, I quite enjoyed my evenings at the FCC as well as high tea with the spirit of Somerset Maugham at The Repulse Bay Hotel on the southern tip of Hong Kong Island. With every well-deserved toast to the *Bang, Bang* team, internally I am also toasting theatre and the arts for always being the place to explore and process the space between personal, professional, political, and societal truth that is the primal fabric of our lives.

Wendy's casting in the play also marked her Hong Kong/Asian debut. This came about through a recommendation from our friend Daisann McLane, who lives in both Hong Kong and New York City. We met Daisann through our mutual friend, theatre auteur Ping Chong, but had long admired her work as the "Frugal Traveler" columnist in the *New York Times*. As a teenager, I also worshipped at Daisann's journalistic feet (and feats) as one of the most prolific rock journalists of that or any era. As a teenager who avidly devoured every column inch of the rock press, I never would have imagined that one day, the author of the *Rolling Stone* cover story on Cheap Trick would recommend my wife for an acting role in Hong Kong!

The night Daisann attended *Bang, Bang* was a most magical night. Also in attendance was Yuet Fung Ho, producer of the film *Freckled Rice*, which was such a life-changer for me—and ultimately led to my devoting my professional life to playwriting and theatre. Yuet was the artistic and life partner of *Freckled Rice*'s director, the late Steve Ning. Over the years we became and stayed friends. A Hong Kong native who also divides her time between Hong Kong and New York City, Yuet was visiting her family during the summer in which Wendy and I were in residence at City U. In addition to her extensive narrative and documentary work in film and television, she was also one of the founders of The Chinatown History Project, which has since bloomed into the Museum of the Chinese in America in New York. Coincidentally, also in attendance that night was a future MOCA president, Nancy Yao Maasbach, who, like me, is a Flushing native! Nancy was based in Hong Kong for many years, and we were introduced to her by Glenn Shive of the Fulbright program, whose informal title should be the great connector of everyone and everything in HK. Proud to say that the night they all attended happened to be one of Wendy and the cast's strongest performances.

After the play, Daisann led us through a maze of back alleys traversing Hong Kong's Central and SoHo districts (South of Hollywood Road) to an old-fashioned speakeasy. This suave retro cocktail lounge, then one of SoHo's best-kept secrets, is accessible only through an unmarked door behind a series of closed-up stalls of one of Hong Kong's omnipresent wet markets. In this unique environment, we hoisted world-class cocktails in numerous toasts to Wendy's Hong Kong debut and inspired return to the stage. Silently, I also toasted our friendships with and inspiration from Daisann and Yuet. If not for these two amazing women, we all may very well have not been doing what we were doing—where we were doing it that night.

After we said our goodbyes, Wendy and I dreamily walked through the humid after-midnight air and the now empty wet market alley. By day, the narrow alley is teeming with loud, colorful fishmongers, produce mongers, and clothing/trinket vendors engaged in highly competitive hard bargaining with hordes of equally loud customers. It had rained earlier in the evening. The humid, post-storm haze hovered over the alley's shimmering, oily puddles and made us feel as if we were walking in a dream. In many ways, we were.

"It's been no bed of roses . . ."
The Last Emperor of Flushing in China

"It's been no bed of roses . . ." Freddie Mercury leads Queen through verse two of "We Are the Champions." In the corner of my eye I see that my late Dad has also entered the *dance-a-bration*. He joins us in our dance but moves in his own orbit—shadowing the circle. He is dressed in the white tuxedo jacket with black slacks, black bow tie, and black cummerbund he wore to make the rounds at the wedding reception of his #1 son, Gene. In our *dance-a-bration*, as he did for the Chinatown wedding guests, Dad holds an opened bottle of Johnnie Walker Red in one hand and a batch of cigars in the other. (You could smoke in New York City restaurants back in 1970.) Thankfully, the City U students cannot access this spirit's open bar.

In Chinese opera and theatre, the spirits and mortals often have a climactic meeting. Spoiler alert for those who may not be familiar with *Our Town* . . . during the play's legendary Act III, which takes place in the Grover's Corners Cemetery, this spirit–mortal meeting takes place when the Stage Manager conjures an opportunity for a newly arrived spirit, that of Emily Webb, to return to her mortal life. Granted this opportunity, Emily exclaims, "I'll choose a happy day," to which a fellow spirit warns, "No! . . . Choose the least important day in your life. It will be important enough."

Such a spirit and mortal "greater good confluence" blessed our workshop for the final and, often, most challenging realm of theatre, and maybe even life, collaboration. At this point in the residency, we asked our City U students to consider merging their scene's characters, acting characterizations, and family research into one narrative, to be titled "Hong Kong Time Capsule 2011." Knowing full well that this experiment in alchemy could easily fail, we devised a "Plan B": to present an evening of short monologues and scenes. As with all prior hurdles, the students cleared this potential obstacle effortlessly and with great camaraderie, humility, and humor. Not unlike their inspiring Grover's Corners counterparts.

As the "greater good" or "all for one" mentality prevailed, the students set about the delicate task of merging their written works and physical creation of characters. Throughout this process, they generously and selflessly rewrote, redirected, and even sacrificed their own stage time and roles to classmates who were better suited for their dramatic sketches—created on the page and stage. During this time, Wendy and I were able to undertake a three-day cultural exchange with the U.S. Consulate, Guangzhou, the capital city of my family's ancestral Guangdong Province—near my family's ancestral village of Toisan. There, I was to perform my memoir monologue play, *The Last Emperor of Flushing*.

The U.S. Consulate, Guangzhou, had a very busy schedule for us. The afternoon before the show, I gave a talk at their weekly forum. It was held in the U.S. Consulate conference room, where, just outside, life-size cardboard figures of President Barack Obama and Secretary of State Hillary Clinton stood sentry . . . it was a wonderful time to be a proud U.S. Fulbright cultural ambassador.

At the U.S. Consulate Forum, a weekly English-language event, I gave a reading of excerpts from *The Last Emperor of Flushing*, and the atmosphere was electric. The audience was hungry for this exchange. The post-reading discussion was one of the most animated I ever had the pleasure of participating in—let alone lead. Some wanted to know about arts and censorship in America, while others wondered about the perception of Chinese in the arts in America. But everyone wanted to know why my play identified so much with China's real life "Last Emperor," Aisin Gioro Pu Yi. I responded that while he may have made many dubious decisions as an adult, we must also remember his innocence as that three-year-old child who ascended the throne of the Qing Dynasty. From there, all agreed, he was mercilessly manipulated as a puppet for the rest of his life. This seemed to satisfy their queries of concern.

Afterward, we met many of the attendees, who are devoted to the consulate's weekly forum. One couple takes their pre-school daughter to the forum every week, aiming to expose her to as much international and progressive stimulus as possible. Then it was on to the evening's performance in Guangzhou's Xiaozhou Village artist district.

Like Shanghai's "Moganshan" and Beijing's "798" arts districts, Guangzhou's Xiaozhou Village arts district is a cluster of galleries and chic cafés in a former industrial and rural village area in a remote part of the city. Xiaozhou Village is a forty-five-minute private drive and an almost two-hour public transport trek from Guangzhou's central Tianhe district. At that time, it was fast becoming the city's cultural center. It is adjacent to University Town and, like China itself, has architectural and cultural elements ranging from the Ming Dynasty to the present day. On the surface, it is a timeless Cantonese village, full of narrow alleyways, canals, and walking bridges, as well as beautiful, well-maintained ancient homes and temples. Elders sit at workstations in front of their homes, sewing, cooking, and tending to daily chores.

Behind, beside, and often carved within these clusters of ancient structures that in northern China are called *hutongs*, the twenty-first century is starting to emerge. During a fascinating walk with Hong Kong/Guangzhou–based translator and playwright Martin Merz, we visited several art galleries, chic cafés, bookstores, and bars in the center of the village. Closer to the outskirts, we saw at least three art schools and corresponding art-supply stores.

Xiaozhou People's Hall is an imposing yellow building that stands just inside the Xiaozhou Village walls. Even in our twenty-first-century heads, these village walls recall ramparts that conjure visions of warring city-states and other divides. Looking at the beautiful trees that line the river and hover over the wall, it is hard to imagine its being a less-than-serene setting when, several centuries prior, the sudden raising of an enemy flag would signal the alarm for full-out attack.

Built in the 1950s, Xiaozhou People's Hall is a national landmark that resonates with history. The red star prominently displayed over the entrance underscores the structure's Soviet-style architecture of that period, as well as its original purpose as a production space during the Great Leap Forward. This means that Xiaozhou People's Hall was originally part factory, part military training base and barracks, and part credit union, among many other things.

As we entered the long, cavernous People's Hall, the Consulate staffers told us that it was also a "hands-on meeting hall" during the tumultuous Cultural Revolution. At the far end of the football field–length meeting area, red-carpeted steps lead to a concrete platform some five feet off the ground. In its day, I imagined, this narrow, 25′ × 5′ platform must have held many a dais full of Chinese Communist Party officials who meted out the current party line. Some twenty-five feet above this platform, another red star presides over a large gold banner featuring giant red Chinese calligraphy. Similar vertical red-on-white banners flank the platform's sides. The staffers told us that these are Chairman Mao's "Great Leap Forward" quotations. The quotes exhort Chinese productivity and ingenuity. It was on this platform that I was to perform in a few hours.

As I stood on the platform, I closed my eyes and tried to imagine the events that had taken place here. Particularly troublesome were thoughts and images of what went on during the "hands-on" Cultural Revolution meetings—the public persecution of artists and intellectuals, many of whom were paraded in the streets wearing dunce caps while being jeered and physically attacked by vicious gangs of Red Guards on the streets. When I opened my eyes, I looked out onto aisles and aisles of paintings and photographs. In 2011, Xiaozhou People's Hall functions primarily as an art gallery and cultural center dedicated to local artists of all genres and disciplines. It would be hard to think of a more positive karmic transition for this formerly notorious space.

That evening's performance of *The Last Emperor of Flushing* was everything I could have hoped for. Many of those in attendance at the Consulate Forum that afternoon, including the precocious pre-school girl and her family, also made what was an almost two-hour public transport trek out to Xiaozhou Village. Every gesture, movement, and word had a newer, deeper meaning in the context of being performed in a city where generations of my ancestors once roamed this Earth.

For several years, I had been performing the solo piece in venues throughout New York City and elsewhere in the United States. During those performances I tried to conjure and convey a sense of the East's impact on a child growing up in an immigrant Chinese American family in the shadows of the Cold War. On stage in Guangzhou, that paradigm shifted. I found myself trying to play and convey the impact of America and the West on a child of Chinese ancestry. In the play's final scene, The Last Emperor of Flushing decides to leave his faux Emperor's robe behind. He takes it off and lays it over his equally faux throne—actually a New York Mets tail-gaiting beach chair—and states:

> Ah yes, I won't be needing this anymore. This belongs to somebody else now. Thank you for sharing these final moments of the Flushing Palace of The Eng Dynasty.

In performances in America this always felt like a bittersweet moment when he was leaving it all behind in order to enter the great beyond behind the walls of his Flushing Palace. On stage in China, it felt like a joyous moment—the conclusion of a journey to bring some of my family's stories home to China. It was also the conclusion of the long journey from longing to belonging—a definitive step in the global expansion of my American frame of reference. Now, as in *Our Town*, our family's hopes and fears, accomplishments and failures, loves lost and found, bought and sold, will forever reverberate in the dark night that emanates from the walls of Xiaozhou Village People's Hall out onto the streets of Guangzhou and beyond.

After the performance and the forty-five-minute private van ride back to central Guangzhou, Martin Merz took us out to an after-hours cabaret in Guangzhou. There, a mischievous young boy with the aura of a provocative eminence or future Dalai

Lama kept eyeing me. Finally, he came over and started asking questions in Mandarin. When I could not give him a response, he reiterated his questions in Cantonese. I still could not muster a response. Finally, he blurted out in perfect English, "You're just a foreigner who looks Chinese!"

In many other times and places, similar dismissive put-downs would have destroyed me. Totally shut me down. But tonight, after my fictitious Emperor persona helped me complete the very real journey of bringing some of our family's stories home to China, I just smiled at the child and laughed with my wife and friends, as well as all of the other spirits in the room that were celebrating this very special night with us.

EPILOGUE

AS THE POST-PERFORMANCE *dance-a-bration* starts its third circle, over regal chorus refrains of "We Are the Champions," the City U students are giving shout-outs for their classmates' favorite moments on stage—both big laughs and big gaffes— that garner huge smiles and raucous applause at this morning-after's *dance-a-bration*.

After a very short writing, devising, and rehearsal period, the City U students masterfully brought their carefully con-structed ensemble play to life. Their confident performances captured every shade of their theatrical portraits of Hong Kong life—written in response to *Our Town*. To evoke *Our Town*, "Hong Kong Time Capsule 2011" utilized minimal lighting, no props, and only a few spare functional pieces of furniture. All eighteen students entered the stage at the beginning and re-mained on stage for the duration of the performance. The students who were not in scenes sat along the stage's perime-ter—creating a malleable ensemble that was a combination of village neighbors, elders, and spirits all rolled into one. At the end of the performance, Wendy and I were in tears and led the audience in a well-deserved standing ovation. With the City U students, we created a new international frame of equal American, Chinese, New York, and Hong Kong sensibilities with which to envision and aspire to a new world. For one night, at least, "we are the champions—of the world" indeed.

As we spin in the *dance-a-bration*, Wendy and I are seeing, feeling, and reciprocating the students' love. In my mind's eye and hands, I also see and feel the love in the eyes and smiling faces of The Empress Mother and Wendy's Mom, Ann Brown, who, as in every day of our lives, hold our hands as we navigate our daily dances through life. Dad is still shadow-orbiting the *dance-a-bration* circle's perimeter. In my mind's ear, "We Are the Champions" is now augmented with aggressive percussion-driven echoes of indigenous Cantonese opera from the land on which we are dancing. The Cantonese opera counterpoint turns Queen's classic rock march into an otherworldly dirge for the dancing spirits of Dad, The Empress Mother, and Ann Brown.

In this moment, I find myself like Emily in *Our Town* during the climactic Act III cemetery scene. In this scene, Emily goes against the warnings of her cemetery-spirit travelers. She accepts the Stage Manager/Trickster's offer to return to the mortal world to simultaneously relive a day from her mortal life, as well as to examine and process this day from her new perspective of a spirit who, just that day, left the world of the living. Emily chooses to revisit her twelfth birthday. After she relives and rewitnesses only the taking of breakfast that morning with her mother and father, her heart is breaking. It pains her to see how young her parents look and how little attention they are paying to each other. Most of all, her heart is breaking with the full acknowledgment of how it all goes by so quickly. Emily immediately begs the Stage Manager/Trickster to end this revisit and return her to the cemetery's spirit world of the afterlife.

During the brief fourteen years that The Empress Mother, Dad, and I were all living together on this planet, I was always silently pleading with my parents, as well as with myself, to actually see and feel each other during our brief dance on Earth. In the back room of our laundry, my parents would blast their Cantonese opera records and I would play The Who's rock opera *Tommy* at a much lower volume. As I listened, I would always imagine myself in the world of *Tommy*. Now, as I visualize Dad and The Empress Mother in the City U *dance-a-bration*, I wonder if my parents also tried to picture themselves in the Cantonese operas they were playing at very loud volumes. Did they see themselves donning the flamboyant costumes and engaging in highly stylized "art of war"-styled dances? Or maybe, through the music, they envisioned opera battles that mirrored the daily battles of their combative arranged marriage.

In some ways, my parents' arranged marriage was the ultimate tragic opera in that I never once saw them dance or engage in any amorous way that went one breath or gesture beyond the bare-bones necessities of running our laundry and our family. In another sense, theirs was an unmitigated immigrant success story in that they both ventured to the other side of the world, at a time when our race was legally blocked from becoming U.S. citizens for almost an entire century, and prospered. Against mountains of societal, institutional, and legal obstacles, they raised five children and maintained a successful Mom-and-Pop Chinese hand laundry business for three decades, as well as two homes.

Seeing my parents spiritually join the City U *dance-a-bration* albeit separately—without physical contact—is as close as I will ever get to seeing them dance together. If this were my Grover's Corners Cemetery moment of *Our Town*, I wonder if I would have been warned against taking this dance with these spirits. But in our Hong Kong Time Capsule 2011, we are not re-creating memories. On last night's stage and this morning's *dance-a-bration*, we are creating new histories.

Now it was time to shout the final iconic chorus refrains of "We Are the Champions" with the City U students. The Empress Mother, Ann Brown, and Dad gracefully exited the circle, bowing and disappearing from the *dance-a-bration*. Most of us still in the circle were dancing with our eyes closed, grasping each other's hands in gratitude for the journey we had just completed and in the full knowledge that we may never see each other again. Throughout our last dance, the students sweetly reprised their ritual of giving us a variety of thumbs-up and peace signs, as well as forming hearts with their hands and an "A" and a "W" with their fingers.

As the final chorus modulated, reprised, and built, I knew that my Dad and The Empress Mother are gone. Wendy's Mom, Ann Brown, is gone . . . but the spirit of the Foo J. Chin Chinese Hand Laundry remains, illuminated by the spirit of *Our Town*. Souls are the reservoir of stories. Stories are the reservoir of lives—present, past, and evermore. Learning to proudly tell my own stories has made me whole.

ACKNOWLEDGMENTS

THE FOUNDATION FOR this memoir began onstage as two solo performance pieces, *The Last Emperor of Flushing* and *The Flushing Cycle*. These works were developed and performed in NYC at Pan Asian Repertory Theatre, Queens Theatre in the Park, and Dixon Place. *The Flushing Cycle* also marked the first time I started creating self-referential work—thanks to Alan Siege, who invited me to participate in a "Tell-a-bration" storytelling marathon "back in the twentieth century." Thank you to all of the "first draft" friends through the years, as well as all of the producers, directors, designers, dramaturgs, and audience members who contributed to the growth and development of these two works. And a big shout-out to my best Flushing/childhood friend, Ray Wong (RIP), who first observed, "You're like The Last Emperor" when I was packing up The Second Flushing Palace in preparing to move out of Flushing.

Thanks to all of the "first draft" and "twenty-first draft" friends and colleagues who read and shared illuminating feedback over the decade-plus gestation process that was the writing of this memoir. Thanks to City Lore (Steve Zeitlin, Amanda Dargan, and Molly Garfinkel) and Think!Chinatown (Amy Chin and Yin Kong) in NYC for hosting public readings and discussions of the memoir-in-progress.

Thanks to Linda Chapman for being such a staunch supporter of this book, and all of the "blurbers" who so generously took the time to read and reflect on the manuscript.

Special thanks: Lanie Lee for copy editing numerous drafts; Louis Chan for advice and assistance on digitizing photos; and to the next generation, my niece, Heather Eng, and second cousin, Skyler Chin, for sharing insightful feedback that truly lifted this book onto higher ground.

Extra special thanks to Janis and Jeff Chan for reading more drafts than they'd probably care to remember. Every time, you both offered invaluable insights.

Heartfelt thanks to Richard Morrison and all at Fordham University Press for giving this book a loving home. Richard has been a steadfast supporter and collaborator throughout the publishing process. Thank you to all of my brother and sister resisters of Rise and Resist for creating an activist community like no other. In this community I met Richard Morrison at an "Immigrant Rights" vigil. Thank you, Mara Hennessey and David Johansen, for introducing my wife, Wendy Wasdahl, and me to Rise and Resist. This was the second time that David changed my life.

Of course, much gratitude, respect, and love to family— biological and chosen—and friends, on this plane and beyond, who have shaped me and whose spirits reverberate throughout this book.

Finally, to my wife, muse, and in-house . . . everything, Wendy Wasdahl. Nothing gets started, developed, or completed without your loving smarts and soulful guidance. I am blessed to share this life with you. To quote "The Genius" of jazz, "Hallelujah, I just love her so!"

Alvin Eng is a native New York City playwright, performer, acoustic punk rock raconteur, and educator. His plays and performances have been seen Off-Broadway, throughout the United States, as well as in Paris, Hong Kong, and Guangzhou, China. Eng is the interviewer/editor of the oral history/play anthology *Tokens? The NYC Asian American Experience on Stage* (Temple University Press/ Asian American Writers' Workshop). His plays, lyrics, and memoir excerpts have also been published in numerous anthologies. Eng's spoken-word videos, songs, storytelling, and commentary have been broadcast and streamed on National Public Radio among others. He is a two-time appointee to the Fulbright Specialists roster of Theatre/ U.S. Studies scholars and a three-time recipient of NYSCA/NYFA Fellowships. His website is www.alvineng.com.

EMPIRE STATE EDITIONS

SELECT TITLES FROM EMPIRE STATE EDITIONS

Britt Haas, *Fighting Authoritarianism: American Youth Activism in the 1930s*

David J. Goodwin, *Left Bank of the Hudson: Jersey City and the Artists of 111 1st Street*. Foreword by DW Gibson

Nandini Bagchee, *Counter Institution: Activist Estates of the Lower East Side*

Susan Celia Greenfield (ed.), *Sacred Shelter: Thirteen Journeys of Homelessness and Healing*

Elizabeth Macaulay-Lewis and Matthew M. McGowan (eds.), *Classical New York: Discovering Greece and Rome in Gotham*

Susan Opotow and Zachary Baron Shemtob (eds.), *New York after 9/11*

Andrew Feffer, *Bad Faith: Teachers, Liberalism, and the Origins of McCarthyism*

Colin Davey with Thomas A. Lesser, *The American Museum of Natural History and How It Got That Way*. Forewords by Neil deGrasse Tyson and Kermit Roosevelt III

Wendy Jean Katz, *Humbug! The Politics of Art Criticism in New York City's Penny Press*

Lolita Buckner Inniss, *The Princeton Fugitive Slave: The Trials of James Collins Johnson*

Mike Jaccarino, *America's Last Great Newspaper War: The Death of Print in a Two-Tabloid Town*

Angel Garcia, *The Kingdom Began in Puerto Rico: Neil Connolly's Priesthood in the South Bronx*

Jim Mackin, *Notable New Yorkers of Manhattan's Upper West Side: Bloomingdale–Morningside Heights*

Matthew Spady, *The Neighborhood Manhattan Forgot: Audubon Park and the Families Who Shaped It*

Robert O. Binnewies, *Palisades: 100,000 Acres in 100 Years*

Marilyn S. Greenwald and Yun Li, *Eunice Hunton Carter: A Lifelong Fight for Social Justice*

Jeffrey A. Kroessler, *Sunnyside Gardens: Planning and Preservation in a Historic Garden Suburb*

Elizabeth Macaulay-Lewis, *Antiquity in Gotham: The Ancient Architecture of New York City*

Ron Howell, *King Al: How Sharpton Took the Throne*

Phil Rosenzweig, *Reginald Rose and the Journey of "12 Angry Men"*

For a complete list, visit www.fordhampress.com/empire-state-editions.